simply
sublime
GIFTS

High-Style, Low-Sew Projects
to Make in a Snap

JODI KAHN

Photography by Scott Jones • Illustrations by Kate Francis

POTTER
CRAFT
New York

For Mom and Dad:
The most giving people I know

Published in the United States by Potter Craft, an imprint of the
Crown Publishing Group, a division of Random House, Inc., New York.
www.crownpublishing.com
www.pottercraft.com

POTTER CRAFT and colophon is a registered trademark of Random House, Inc.

Library of Congress Cataloging-in-Publication Data

Kahn, Jodi.
  Simply sublime gifts : high-style, low-sew projects to make in a snap / Jodi
Kahn ; photography by Scott Jones ; illustrations by Kate Francis.
    p. cm.
  Includes index.
  ISBN 978-0-307-46446-0
  1. Needlework. 2. Sewing. I. Title.
  TT750.K22 2010
  746.4--dc22
                                        2009046773

Printed in China

Design by Chi Ling Moy
Photography by Scott Jones/www.scottjonesphotography.com
Illustrations by Kate Francis/Brown Bird Design

10 9 8 7 6 5 4 3 2 1

First Edition

acknowledgments

I feel so lucky to have been able to write this book, which couldn't have happened without the help, support, encouragement and hard work from dozens and dozens of people. First and foremost, thank you Andy Barzvi, agent extraordinaire and just all around adorable person! I always want you on my team. And a big huge thank you to my great team at Potter Craft: Betty Wong, Rebecca Behan, Chi Ling Moy, Kim Small, Thom O'Hearn, and Victoria Craven, and also to Kevin Kosbab and Nancy Sabato. You guys rock! Thank you for your dedication and unerring eyes, and for stitching together all the pieces into something that feels virtually seamless.

This book's two unsung heroes are my photographer and illustrator. Scott Jones, your photos make me swoon and are the heart and soul of this book. Thank you for being my partner once again. Kate Francis, how did I ever get lucky enough to work with you? Your illustrations are just flat out fantastic, and you win the patience award. Thank you both for making this book what it is.

A gigantic thank you (and hug) to my gorgeous models and generous friends who shared their homes, shops, and expertise with me: Gary Belsky; Danielle Burrows; Kyle and Andrés de Lasa; Jackson Jones; Ruby Jones; Hannah Kahn; Sam Kahn; Andy Lachow; Hannah Lachow; Ann and Rick Lefever; Elizabeth, Kristen, and Kevin McCarthy; Lauren and Suzanne McGrath and Jack and Patrick Reilly; Alexandra Peters; Nancy Rosenberger at the Quilt Cottage; Maya Samach; Tammy Santacruz; Fran Schreibman from Blondie's Treehouse; and Jill Simpson.

A special thank you to Leah Doyle and Peter Coleman. The warmth and beauty of your home lit up more than half the photos in this book. Thank you from the bottom of my heart.

And most of all, thank you to my friends and family for living through this (and putting up with me!) again. I am so blessed to have your love and support. You all are the greatest gifts I could ever ask for—David, Sam, and Hannah, you are at the top of that list.

2

pretty presents
Gifts for Her

1

hostess with the mostest
Hostess Gifts

3

it's a guy thing
Gifts for Him

introduction

The best presents I've ever received (or given!) have been handmade. My sister gave me a hand-sewn quilt when I got married, and my aunt knit me a lacy baby blanket when my son Sam was born. And I smile every time I see the ceramic purse-shaped planter that my daughter Hannah made for me after I wrote my first craft book, *Simply Sublime Bags*. These presents are treasures. They are beautiful in their own right—the intricate stitching on the lace blanket, for example, is almost miraculous! But the value of these gifts goes way beyond their surface appeal.

When I started writing this book, I gave a lot of thought to why these handmade presents mean so much. I think the notion that someone would take the time to make a gift by hand, and then be willing to give it away, is part of the reason. When someone makes something especially for you, it feels like you're getting a little piece of that person along with the gift. And handmade gifts are, by nature, truly unique. So when you're looking to give something special, what better way than to make it yourself?

Nowadays, trying to find the perfect gift is practically a weekly occurrence. Did you know that one of the top phrases people search for on Google is "gift ideas"? It seems like we're always looking for some kind of present: a hostess gift, birthday present, or just a little token to say, "I love you." This book is filled with dozens of homemade gift ideas that you can whip up for friends, family, teachers, and just about anyone else in your life who deserves a special treat. The ideas are meant to take the pressure off—so you can focus on the fun of making and giving instead of worrying about *what* to give.

The chapters are arranged by types of gifts: Hostess Gifts, Gifts for Her, Gifts for Him, Gifts for Kids, Gifts from the Heart, and Gifts of the Season. As with *Simply Sublime Bags*, many of the projects in this book are made from accessible, recycled or repurposed materials. For example, the Wonder-ful Apron in Chapter 1 (page 17) uses recycled Wonder Bread wrappers to turn kitchen chores into kitschy good fun. Cozy dishtowels make the slippers on page 37 a cinch to whip up and comfy to wear. Many projects allow you to utilize your favorite fabrics and small scraps you might have on hand, such as the Fabric Note Cards on page 102 and the Fabric Nesting Bowls on page 106.

Each project includes a list of supplies needed and is accompanied by icons that show you whether the project is no-sew, low-sew, or requires hand sewing, and whether it can be made with recycled materials. A sewing machine will make many projects quicker and easier to complete, but many of them can be sewn completely by hand if desired.

In addition, all the projects in the book are rated on a difficulty scale of 1–5, but don't let those level 5s scare you. Illustrations guide you through each project every step of the way. Throughout the book, you'll also find super-easy "It's a Snap" projects. These presents can be made in just a few quick steps because, as we all know, time isn't always on our side! The pretty linen hand towels on page 14, for example, look like they've been individually silk-screened, but can actually be made using commercial gift wrap and iron-on transfer paper in less than half an hour!

The presents in this book may be handmade, but they're also loaded with style, so don't forget to complement your creations with clever gift tags and gift-wrapping. After all, presentation is part of the package, and pretty wrapping can elevate a simple pot holder or pincushion to a truly one-of-a-kind gift. Several gift-wrapping ideas are sprinkled throughout the book, offering more ways to flex your creative muscle.

Whether you're looking for a last-minute gift idea or a chance to challenge your inner designer, my hope is that the projects in the book will serve as jumping-off points for your own creativity. Feel free to embellish, tweak, and combine ideas. And of course, if you find a project you really like, make a bunch! It's great to have some handmade gifts stashed away and ready to go at a moment's notice. (And of course, make some for yourself, too!) Most important, remember to have fun! Your joy will shine through, and the results will be *simply sublime*.

icon key

 NO-SEW Amazing, but true! You can make these projects without threading a needle or sewing a single stitch.

 HAND-SEWN Putting the "hand" back in "handmade." These projects are easily completed with a little hand sewing.

 LOW-SEW Machine stitching required but usually nothing that will burn out your Bernina.

 RECYCLE Eco-friendly projects made from reused materials—go green!

 IT'S A SNAP Perfect last-minute gift ideas. These projects can be made in a snap (and in just a few steps).

project skill level

 LEVEL 1 For the DIY newbie: These projects require very little time or materials.

 LEVEL 2 Still easy peasy, with some basic skills introduced.

 LEVEL 3 You're crafting now! But don't worry . . . these projects will still take just an hour or two.

LEVEL 4 You'll earn some street cred after finishing one of these projects. More challenging, but still doable in an afternoon.

LEVEL 5 Craftalicious! Your family won't be able to use the dining-room table for a while, but it'll be worth it!

supply closet

You can whip up most of the gifts in this book with just a few basic supplies (scissors, pins, tape measure, white glue, duct tape, sewing machine, and thread). But stocking up on a few additional items will make the projects even easier. And besides, having a fully equipped sewing or craft area is every gal's dream, right?

Here's a list of some of the best tools and supplies to have on hand:

scissors and cutting tools

Investing in the right cutting tools is well worth it; a good pair of scissors or pinking shears can last a lifetime. And if at all possible, purchase a rotary cutter and self-healing mat, too. You will use them in countless ways, trust me!

- Good pair of 8" (20.5cm) shears
- Ordinary craft scissors for cutting paper
- Second pair of craft scissors for cutting tape (or Teflon scissors)
- Small, sharp embroidery scissors
- Pinking shears
- Seam ripper (we all make mistakes!); also good for punching small holes and making slits
- Rotary cutter and self-healing mat (optional)

* TAPE TIP

Using tape in place of pins or basting stitches is one of my favorite sewing shortcuts. But the subtle differences in types of tape can have a big impact on your sewing machine. If you plan to sew over tape, choose a matte-finish version, such as Scotch "Magic" tape. Compared to clear cellophane tape, this tape is easier to stitch over and remove. It is a little less sticky, and therefore will not gunk up your sewing machine the way other tapes can. You'll still need to take care when sewing over tape; clean or change your needle when a residue builds up.

measuring tools

- Tape measure
- Regular 12" (30.5cm) ruler
- Yardstick
- Acrylic ruler (optional, to be used with rotary cutter and mat)

tape

- Masking tape
- 1/2" (13mm) double-sided tape
- White duct tape
- Matte-finish tape, such as Scotch "Magic" tape
- Clear cellophane tape

stapler and staples

- Heavy-duty desk stapler
- Standard metal staples

glue

- Ordinary white craft glue
- Spray adhesives (such as Spray Mount Adhesive)
- Fabric glue (such as Fabri-Tac or Gem-Tac)

pins and pincushions

- Dressmaker pins
- Ordinary safety pins or quilter's safety pins
- Pincushion
- Wrist-style pincushion (not strictly necessary, but I can't live without mine!)

needles and thimble

- Assorted hand-sewing needles
- Curved quilt needle
- Embroidery needle
- Assorted needles for your machine
- Comfortable thimble

thread

- Assorted threads (all-purpose mercerized cotton-wrapped polyester thread is good for most projects)
- Embroidery floss in a few colors

before you get started

· · · · · · · · · · · · · · · · · ·

Before you begin a project, read through the entire supply list and instructions. Nothing is more frustrating than getting knee-deep into a project and finding out that you're missing one or two key ingredients. Unless otherwise noted, fabric dimensions are listed as width by height, followed by their metric equivalent. For example, a piece of fabric that is 10" wide and 25" high will be listed as 10" x 25" (25.5cm x 63.5cm). And finally, unless directed otherwise, use a straight stitch when sewing with a machine, trimming all threads when you're done.

ironing equipment

- Steam iron
- Ironing board (for ironing and as an extra work space)
- Cotton press cloth
- Baker's parchment paper (to use when ironing plastic materials)
- Transfer papers (Fun with Fabric Transfers, this page)

marking tools

- Ordinary #2 pencil
- Black permanent marker (such as a Sharpie)
- White marking pencil (optional)
- Dressmaker's tracing paper (optional)

sewing machine

Although not strictly necessary, a sewing machine will make some projects quicker and easier to complete. A walking-foot attachment may be helpful at times (individual pattern instructions will call for it where useful).

personal computer, scanner, and printer

Several projects involve using a computer, scanner, or printer. In most cases, a copy store can assist you if you do not have this equipment at home (see individual pattern instructions).

fun with fabric transfers

Several of the gifts in the book use some sort of transfer paper or other iron-on product. These fun materials will allow you to push the limits of what you can create with fabric, and will also let you incorporate favorite photos and images into your projects. Transfer papers can be found at art supply and fabric stores, and often even at office supply stores and large chains like Target and Wal-Mart. Transfer papers can also be purchased online.

As you shop for materials, you'll find many types of papers and brands to choose from. I've had great luck with products made by June Tailor and iron-on vinyls made by Therm O Web (Resources, page 118). Use the guidelines below to help you choose just the right product for your needs. Remember that ironing times, washability, and so on will vary from brand to brand, and that it's always a good idea to test a new product before using it on your final project.

T-SHIRT TRANSFER PAPER These allow you to transfer photos or other images onto fabric using a hot iron. Several 8½" x 11" (21.5cm x 28cm) sheets come in a package. Usually made for inkjet printers (although I have also seen transfer paper for laser printers available online), with these transfers you can print photos or graphics directly from your computer onto the transfer sheet. The transfer is applied face down, then ironed onto the fabric, so you must print your design onto the transfer paper in reverse, or mirror image, for it to come out correctly on the finished product. Unless otherwise noted, basic T-shirt transfer paper is meant to be used with light-colored fabrics and is machine washable after application.

T-SHIRT TRANSFER PAPER FOR DARK FABRICS Like regular T-shirt transfer paper, you can print photos or graphics directly from your computer onto the transfer sheet using your color inkjet printer. However, these transfers are ironed on face up, directly onto fabric. (A piece of parchment paper is included, which is placed on top of the transfer to protect your iron.) Therefore, you won't need to print out mirror images of your designs. Also, these transfers are "thicker" and more opaque than transparent transfers for light colored fabric.

You can use transfers for dark fabrics in a variety of ways. For example, in the Washroom Bag project (page 68), the blank transfer paper is cut into a fun shape and then ironed onto the bag like a decal.

PRINTABLE FABRIC SHEETS This is one of my favorite products! These prepared fabric sheets can be put through an inkjet printer, allowing you to print out any design or photo from your computer directly onto a paper-backed piece of fabric. Different products have various ways for making the design colorfast, but often it can be "heat set" using a hot iron. Depending on what product you use, your material may be hand-washable or need to be dry-cleaned.

You can also make your own fabric sheets using light- or medium-weight fabric with freezer paper or full-sheet adhesive labels as "backing paper." (See page 55 for instructions on how to make your own printable fabric sheets.)

IRON-ON VINYL Another fun product, iron-on vinyl allows you to easily "laminate" material. Not only will the vinyl make the material water resistant, it is also a great way to add some heft to material, almost like an easy iron-on interfacing or lining.

hostess with the mostest

hostess gifts

I am always thrilled when the need for a hostess gift arises. It means that someone is going to cook for me (or put clean sheets on their guest bed for me!), so I'm only too happy to bring a gift! And not only is bringing a hostess gift the nice thing to do, it's the right thing to do. According to Emily Post, the doyenne of etiquette, when going to dinner at someone else's house you should come bearing a small token of appreciation, ideally something that doesn't take too much of the hostess's time or attention. (For example, if you bring flowers, Post suggests that they're already cut and in a vase.)

The projects in this chapter range in difficulty from "it's a snap" easy to "keep you on your toes" challenging, but all of them will help you say thank you in style. And although these gifts are organized with the hostess in mind, you'll probably find a lot of other willing recipients for the projects in this chapter. So even if you're without a dinner invite at the moment, don't wait to start making these presents—when word gets out about what you're cooking up, the invitations are sure to pour in!

Handy Hand Towels

finished measurements

14" x 22" (35.5cm x 56cm)

supplies

- Wrapping paper, 8½" x 11" (21.5cm x 28.cm) sheet or larger

- Scissors and ruler (or rotary cutter and self-healing mat)

- Scanner and printer

- 2 sheets T-shirt transfer paper

- 2 blank guest towels, each approximately 14" x 22" (35.5cm x 56cm)

- Iron and ironing board

- Silk ribbon, for wrapping

These pretty hand towels are my go-to gift when I'm invited to someone's house for dinner. After all, who couldn't use a new set of hand towels, especially ones that look so elegant, and happen to be surprisingly easy and inexpensive to make? Once you have your supplies on hand, you can turn out a whole batch of these in less than half an hour.

The intricate patterns on the towels look like carefully silk-screened designs, but are actually made using wrapping paper and iron on T-shirt transfers. Undecorated linen towels, often called embroidery blanks, are easy to find online and at craft stores at minimal cost. And any wrapping-paper scrap will do, although designs with a white background work especially well. Just one bit of advice: Make a few extra sets of these to stash away for emergency last-minute gifts—you won't believe how often they come in handy!

1. Cut out an 8½" x 11" (21.5cm x 28cm) piece of wrapping paper, then scan and print the image directly onto a T-shirt transfer sheet. (If you don't have a scanner, a copy store can scan and print out the image for you.)

2. After you've printed your image, isolate the design you want to feature and cut it out. If you'd like your design to go across the entire bottom of the towel, you will need to cut 2 matching strips, which will then be pieced together on the bottom of the towel to form one long design.

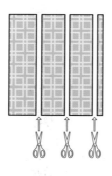

A rotary cutter and self-healing mat work well for this.

3. Before ironing, figure out exactly where you want the strips to go by placing them right side up on the towel. Trim the 2 strips as needed so the design lines up and looks like it is continuous and fits inside the width of the towel.

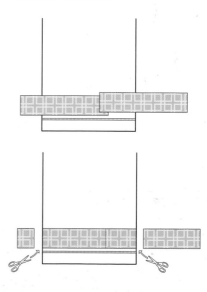

4. Iron the blank towel to get out all the wrinkles. Then, following the directions on the T-shirt transfer package, iron the images onto the towel, one strip at a time. Remember to place images face down on the towel. Place the second strip right next to the first strip so the designs line up and look like they are seamless. Remove the backing from the transfer.

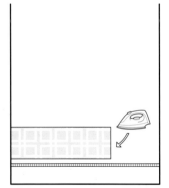

5. Tie up your towels with a silk ribbon to add a finishing touch. That's it!

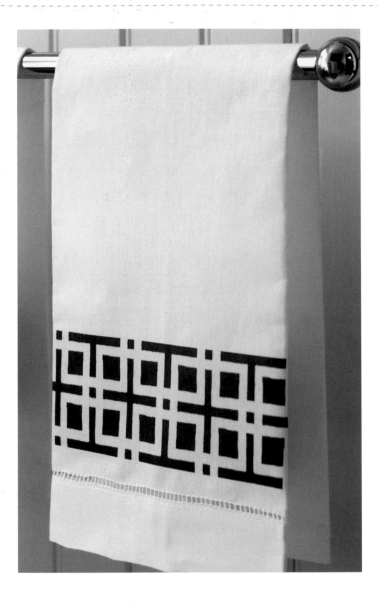

✽ FAUX SILK-SCREENING

To achieve a satiny, silk-screened finish, remove the transfer's backing paper immediately after ironing, without waiting for it to cool completely. Do, however, make sure the image has transferred successfully first. If part of the image pulls up and is still stuck to the transfer paper, place the paper back down, and iron again for another 30—40 seconds.

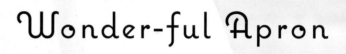

Wonder-ful Apron

Wonder-ful Apron

finished measurements
17" x 20¼" (43cm x 51.5cm)

supplies

- 1 yard (91cm) white broadcloth
- Sewing machine and white thread
- Iron and ironing board
- 4 Wonder Bread wrappers
- Parchment paper

When my daughter Hannah was little, she noticed everything. She counted the spots on ladybugs she found in the yard and noticed when the moon was out in the daytime. Through her eyes, I saw things I hadn't noticed in a long time and started looking at ordinary things in new ways—things like the colorful balloon graphics on a loaf of Wonder Bread!

I've wanted to make something out of Wonder Bread wrappers for years and finally decided on a kitschy kitchen apron. When I first set out to use the wrappers, I thought about laminating or taping them to make "plastic fabric." But the material turned out stiff and lumpy. I started experimenting and found I could "melt" the wrappers directly onto the fabric. I was so excited about my discovery; I tried ironing other plastic wrappers onto cloth and found that Wonder Bread wrappers, for some reason, work much better than most. I guess it's just one more thing that makes this iconic sandwich bread especially wonder-ful. Enjoy!

1. Cut the pieces for the apron out of the broadcloth.
   Main apron panel:
   36" x 20" (91cm x 51cm)
   Apron ties (cut 2):
   36" x 6" (91cm x 15cm)
   Waistband: 20" x 6" (51cm x 15cm)

2. Hem the side and bottom edges of the main apron panel: With *wrong side up*, hem one side edge by folding over ⅜" (9mm) of fabric. Press, then fold over again ⅜" (9mm) and press. Stitch the hem down by sewing close to the folded edge. Repeat on remaining side edge.

   Hem the bottom: Hem the bottom edge in the same manner, but instead turn over ⅝" (1.5cm) and then another ⅝" (1.5cm). Iron and sew down close to the folded edge.

   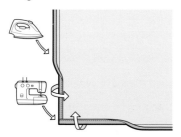

3. Prepare the Wonder Bread wrappers: You will use 2 wrappers for the front of the apron and 2 for the waistband. For the front, slice open a Wonder Bread bag down one side seam only. Open the bag flat so you have 2 polka dot sections. Trim around the sections to get the shape you want, leaving the 2 sections attached to each other. Repeat with another wrapper. Lay the wrappers next to each other on the bottom of the main apron panel, on the right side of the fabric, just inside and above the hemmed edges. Trim wrappers near side edges so they fit nicely in the space, with a little extra room on each edge.

4. Iron a sample: Iron a scrap of the wrapper to an extra piece of broadcloth to test the adhering process. Set the iron on the highest setting. Use a piece of parchment paper to completely cover the plastic wrapper and protect your iron. Iron the wrapper, right side up, onto the fabric, holding the iron over the image for about 10 seconds at a time, moving the iron around to avoid scorching the image. Repeat this process a few times until the wrapper adheres completely. Let the parchment paper cool before pulling it back to check if wrapper has adhered. If the wrapper has not adhered completely, iron a little longer.

   Note: If you pull parchment paper off completely, and need to reiron, use a new, clean piece of parchment paper.

5. Iron the wrappers to the apron: Once you've tested the process, apply the wrappers to the main apron panel in the same manner, applying one wrapper at a time, and always keeping parchment paper over the entire image to protect your iron and keep the image from melting.

   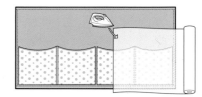

6. Iron wrappers to the waistband section: Cut the remaining 2 wrappers and arrange them so they completely cover the waistband section. Trim the wrappers so they do not hang over the fabric edge. Iron the wrappers onto the waistband, as described in step 4. When cool, remove the parchment paper and trim the waistband fabric to 18" x 5" (45.5cm x 12.5cm).

   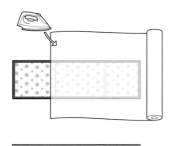

   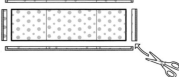

7. Gather the main apron panel: Using a long basting stitch, sew across the top of the apron panel using a ⅜" (9mm) seam allowance, and then again using a ¼" (6mm) seam allowance. Pull the threads to gather the top so it measures approximately 17" (43cm) across.

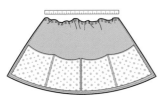

8. Add the waistband: Beginning ½" (13mm) in on the waistband edge, and with right sides together, pin the long, raw edge of the waistband to the top of the gathered apron panel. (The extra ½" [13mm] of waistband at each end of the apron panel will provide the seam allowance for attaching the ties.) Sew the waistband to the apron, using a ½" (13mm) seam allowance and backstitching at each end. Fold back waistband so it is right side up. Then, fold over ½" (13mm) along the raw waistband edge toward the wrong side of the waistband and press.

Note: Before pressing, use 2 pieces of parchment paper to cover the front and the back of the waistband to protect the fabric, iron, and ironing board.

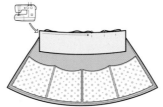

9. Make the ties: With right sides together, fold the first tie in half lengthwise, and pin in place. Using a ½" (13mm) seam allowance, sew down the long side raw edges and around one end, leaving the other end open. Clip the sewn corner on an angle to facilitate turning. Turn tie right side out, and press. Repeat to make the remaining tie.

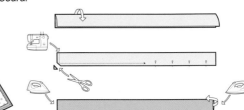

10. Make pleats in the ties: Fold a tie in half lengthwise. At the unfinished end, sew a small, ⅝"-(1.5cm-) long seam ¼" (6mm) from the fold to create a pleat. Repeat on the remaining tie. Open up both ties and lay flat.

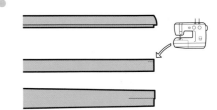

11. Attach the ties to the waistband: With the apron and attached waistband *right side* up, line up the pleated end of one tie with the raw end of the waistband (begin with the left side first).

up, up, and away!

• • • • • • • • • • • •

In 1921, Taggart Baking Company executive Elmer Cline was visiting the International Balloon Race at the Indianapolis Speedway, where the sky was filled with hundreds of colorful balloons. To Elmer, the image signified a sense of "wonder" and was the catalyst for naming the company's new product, a 1½-pound (680g) loaf of white bread, Wonder Bread. In 1925, Wonder Bread became the country's first precut loaf, changing the American sandwich forever and inspiring the phrase "best thing since sliced bread."

Make sure that the pleat on the tie opens toward the bottom edge of the apron, and that the long sewn edge of the tie lines up at the seam connecting the waistband to the apron. Pin in place, and then baste the tie to the waistband using a ⅜" (9mm) seam allowance.

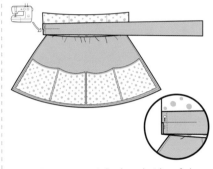

Repeat on right-hand side of the apron with the remaining tie.

Now fold the waistband in half, over the ties, lining up the side raw edges. Pin the sides together, then sew using a ½" (13mm) seam allowance, backstitching at each end.

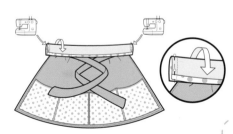

12. Turn the waistband right side out, pulling out both of the ties. Then turn the apron over so the wrong side is facing up. Finger-press the waistband flat and carefully pin the folded waistband edge so it covers the raw gathered edge and lines up with the waistband seam.

Be careful not to poke pins all the way through the front of the waistband, as they can leave holes in the polka-dot fabric.

Turn the apron back over so the *right* side is facing up. Topstitch the waistband very close to the bottom edge to finish the waistband, back-stitching at each end, and carefully removing the pins from the underside of the fabric as you sew.

✳ WASH BUT DON'T DRY

To keep this apron wonder-ful, wash it in cold water on a gentle cycle, and hang it up to dry.

Make yourself a sandwich, put your feet up, and relax! You've earned it.

Hello Cupcake! Pincushion

finished measurements
2¾" x 3" (7cm x 7.5cm)

supplies

- Cupcake pattern templates (page 120)

- Two 9" x 12" (23cm x 30.5cm) squares of felt (one to match the silicone base, and another color for the felt "frosting")

- Needle and thread in colors to match the felt and the decorations

- 2¾"- (7cm-) diameter silicone baking cup (Resources, page 118)

- Scrap of T-shirt fabric, approximately 6" x 6" (15cm x 15cm)

- Polyester fiberfill craft stuffing

- Rickrack, buttons, beads, small pom-poms and other notions for decorations

What is it about cupcakes that makes them so irresistible? Cupcakes have never been hotter, and these little hand-sewn pincushions are the perfect gift for anyone who is cupcake obsessed, whether they sew or not! A colorful silicone cupcake liner is used as the base and gives this felt confection a realistic look. The sky's the limit when it comes to decorating; rickrack becomes frosting, buttons become candies, and beads transform into brightly colored sprinkles on top of these felt treats. But watch out, these cupcakes are truly addictive. Luckily they are also fat and calorie free—they just *look* good enough to eat!

1. Make the felt bottom: Photocopy the cupcake pattern templates at the recommended percentage, and cut out the paper patterns. Use the patterns to cut out a cupcake base bottom and side from the felt matching the color of the silicone cup. The cupcake base will fit inside the silicone cup and will not be seen when the cupcake is complete.

2. Form cupcake base: Line up the cupcake base bottom edge with the lower cupcake base side edge and begin to hand-stitch them together using a scant ⅛" (3mm) seam allowance. Ease the curved side edges around the round cupcake bottom, but do not sew the side edges together.

Place the felt base into the silicone baking cup to check the fit. Make any necessary adjustments so the felt base fits nicely inside the silicone cup, then stitch up the side edges. Trim any extra material at the edges and remove felt base from the baking cup.

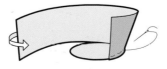

3. Make base top: Using the cupcake base top pattern template, cut out the top from a scrap of T-shirt fabric. Using a needle and thread, hand-stitch around the circle using a long running stitch and about a ¼" (6mm) seam allowance. Before knotting the thread end, pull the thread to gather the fabric and form what will look like a little shower cap. (To check how tight you should gather the stitches, turn the top so that the stitches are face up, and use the cupcake bottom as a guide: The base bottom should fit just inside the gathers.) Tighten or loosen stitches as needed, and then knot the thread to hold the gathers in place.

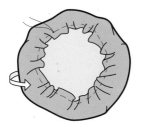

4. Stuff the little "cap" very tightly with the fiberfill stuffing, and place a handful of stuffing in the bottom of the base as well. Then place the stuffed cupcake top into the base, and baste the top into place using a long running stitch. Keep the stitches as far below the top edge of the felt base piece as possible so they'll be hidden when the felt cupcake sits inside the baking cup. As you stitch, periodically place the base into the baking cup to check the proportions.

5. Make the "frosted" felt top: Cut out a "frosting" swirl from contrasting felt using the cupcake frosting pattern template. Start pinning the layers of the felt swirl

together so it forms a cone top. Once you've got the shape you want, place it on top of the stuffed cupcake to make sure it fits. Remove the swirl from the stuffed cupcake and, using a tiny stitch, tack the layers of the felt swirl in place every ½" (13mm) or so, leaving the threads loose between stitches on the inside of the felt swirl. If you pull the thread tightly between stitches the felt cone swirl will not fit over the stuffed cupcake.

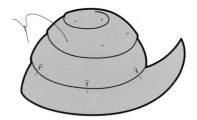

6. Before you sew the felt frosting onto the cupcake base, decorate it with buttons, pom-poms, or other notions. Rickrack trim is easier to apply after the frosting has been attached.

7. Sew the frosting swirl to the felt cupcake bottom: Using tiny stitches, sew through the frosting, and then through the felt cupcake bottom, continuing around the cupcake until the frosting has been completely sewn on. Keep the stitches on the frosting part as small as possible, but don't worry too much about the stitches showing on the felt base; they will be hidden inside the silicone cup.

8. Once the felt frosting is completely sewn on, place the fabric cupcake into the silicone base. Sew the silicone cup to the cupcake at the bottom by poking the needle and thread through the cupcake first, then through the silicone cup, tacking the cupcake down in a few places, then pulling the thread tight so that the cupcake sits firmly in the baking cup.

Add rickrack or other trim by tacking it into place around the lower edge of the frosting with tiny stitches.

Icing on the Cake

Wrap your cupcake in a little bakery box tied with bakeshop twine. Your hostess will eat it up!

Hot Stuff Pot Holder and Oven Mitt

finished measurements

square pot holder—8" x 8" (20.5cm x 20.5cm); oven mitt—6½" x 12¼" (16.5cm x 31cm)

supplies

- 1 quilted moving blanket, approximately 72" x 82" (183cm x 208cm), or other thick, quilted fabric (Resources, page 118)

- Scissors and ruler (or rotary cutter, straightedge, and self-healing mat)

- ½ yard (45.5cm) contrasting fabric for pocket and oven mitt trim

- Sewing machine and a ⁹⁰⁄₁₄ or ¹⁰⁰⁄₁₆ needle for heavy material

- Thread

- Pins

- 1 package (4 yards [3.7m]) ½"- (13mm-) wide double-fold bias tape in contrasting color

- Iron and ironing board

- Oven mitt pattern template (page 121)

- 1" (2.5cm) bias-tape-making tool (Optional. The 1" [2.5cm] tool makes tape that can be folded into ½"- [13mm-] wide double-fold tape. Refer to Making Your Own Bias Tape, page 31.)

I've been obsessed with quilted mover's blankets for a long time. I love seeing piles of the multicolored pads stacked up in the back of the moving van, or covering furniture as it gets shuttled off to a new destination. It's something about the colors and texture—the blankets are clearly utilitarian, but have you ever noticed that they often come in very earthy shades? Kind of like the hues of natural dyed wool?

You can find quilted moving blankets at many hardware stores or at a local moving company. I got mine at a mover's supply house in the Bronx (Resources, page 118) and landed a huge blanket for less than $15. I decided to whip up a bunch of cute pot holders from the multi-layered, pre-quilted fabric, saving a lot of cutting and sewing time and allowing me to focus on the fun part: making loads of presents in a flash. One blanket will provide enough material for twenty to thirty pot holders—that's a whole year's worth of hostess gifts!

Square Pot Holder

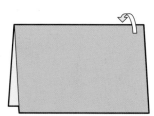

1. Cut out an 8" x 8" (20.5cm x 20.5cm) square from the quilted blanket and an 8" x 11" (20.5cm x 28cm) piece of contrasting fabric for the pocket.

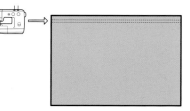

2. Prepare the pocket: With wrong sides together, fold the contrasting fabric in half to form an 8" x 5½" (20.5cm x 14cm) rectangle. Topstitch ⅜" (9mm) from the fold, and then again very near the folded edge to finish the top of the pocket. Pin the pocket to the front of the blanket fabric, aligning the raw edges, then baste in place along the sides only using a ⅜" (9mm) seam allowance.

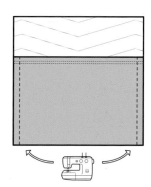

3. Add the bias tape: Cut a 56" (142cm) length of bias tape and open up and flatten out the *smaller* of the folded edges. With the right sides together, line up the raw edge of the bias tape on the front of the pot holder so it is almost flush with the top, left edge. Then begin pinning the bias tape to the pot holder, starting at the upper left corner.

Note: You may need to play around with where you place the bias tape to neatly cover the thick quilted fabric without a gap. The goal is to be able to stitch the bias tape in place on the front of the pot holder using a 1/2" (13mm seam) allowance. For further instructions refer to How to Apply Bias Tape, opposite.

Sew the first side of the tape in place, using a 1/2" (13mm) seam allowance and stopping 1/2" (13mm) from the first side edge, backstitching at the beginning and end of the seam.

4. Make a mitered corner: Fold the binding away from the pot holder at a 90-degree angle (the corner will form a 45-degree angle), then fold the tape back so it is lined up with the raw edge of the next side. Pin in place along the second side. Begin stitching 1/2" (13mm) from the edge, stopping 1/2" (13mm) from the end of the second side. Repeat this step all the way around, but do not miter the last corner; this is where you will make the loop. Trim all loose threads.

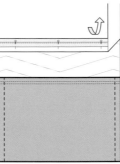

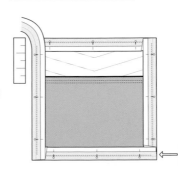

5. Fold the bias tape over the raw edge of the pot holder to finish all edges, pinning in place and folding the corners on the back so that they are also mitered. Topstitch the bias tape on the front of the pot holder, close to the edge where the folded bias tape meets the pot holder. Make sure you are "catching" the bias tape on the back. At the end, continue stitching the extra bias tape closed.

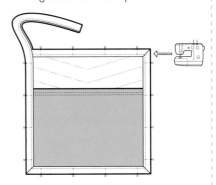

6. Make the loop: With the pot holder right side up, fold the extra tape back to the left to form a loop. Fold under the raw edge of loop, and then pin it in place on the back of the pot holder. Stitch the loop in place, stitching directly over the line of topstitching on the bias tape.

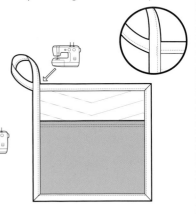

Oven Mitt

1. Photocopy the oven mitt pattern template at the recommended percentage, and cut out the paper pattern. Fold the blanket with right sides together, and use the pattern to cut out two pieces of the blanket for the mitt.

2. Make your own bias binding: For this project, you will only need to make a small amount of bias tape, approximately 26" (66cm) long. (To make longer pieces, refer to Making Your Own Bias Tape, page 31.) Begin by folding your fabric on a diagonal, taking one of the selvage edges and lining it up with one of the cut edges so the fold is at a 45-degree angle. The folded fabric will be shaped like a triangle. With the fabric still folded, measure over 1" (2.5cm) from the fold, and cut using a straightedge (this will give you a 2"- [5cm-] wide strip when the fabric is unfolded).

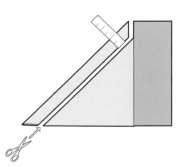

how to apply bias tape

• • • • • • • • • • • • • • • •

1. Open up the folded bias tape so the smaller of the folded sides is opened flat.

2. With right sides together, line up the crease from the fold you just opened with the seam line on the fabric you are planning to stitch. (Again, make sure that the smaller, narrow side of the bias tape is closest to seam.) Sew, tape side up, along the creased line.

3. Clip curves of fabric if necessary, then fold the bias tape back over the raw edge of the fabric and pin in place.

4. Topstitch the bias tape in place on the front of the item you are sewing, close to the edge where the folded bias tape meets the other fabric. Be careful to make sure that you are catching the bias tape on the back.

Fold the strip lengthwise with wrong sides together, and press. Open up the strip, and using the center line as your guide, fold both raw edges in toward the center crease and press in place (a bias tape tool is very helpful for this). Fold tape in half again along the original center crease to create ½"- (13mm-) wide folded tape. Press.

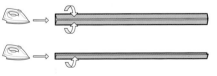

3. Assemble the oven mitt: With right sides together, pin the oven

mitt pieces together. Start sewing on the side of the mitt without the thumb, using a ½" (13mm) seam allowance. Stitch about two-thirds around the oven mitt, stopping just after you sew most of the thumb. Backstitch at the beginning and end of the seam.

At the bottom, where you started your seam, trim the seam allowance to ¼" (6mm).

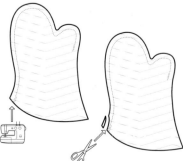

4. Add the bias tape: Open the bottom of the mitt so there is a continuous, curved bottom edge. Open one edge of the folded tape, and with right sides together, line up the raw edge of the unfolded side of the tape with the raw edge of the bottom of the mitt. Leave about 1" (2.5cm) of extra tape at the beginning. Pin the tape in place along the bottom edge and then stitch the tape in place using a scant ½" (13mm) seam allowance. (Because your homemade bias tape has 2 equal folded sides, using just slightly less than a ½" [13mm] seam allowance will help the bias tape fold over neatly and allow you to "catch" the back side of the tape when you sew it in place.)

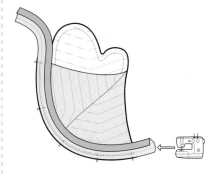

5. Fold the tape over to cover the raw edge of the oven mitt bottom and pin in place. Topstitch on the right side of the mitt on

the tape, close to where the bias tape meets the mitt fabric, making sure to catch the tape on the other side. When you reach the end of the mitt, keep stitching the extra bias tape together. This end will become your loop.

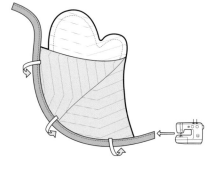

6. Make the loop: Fold the extra bias tape toward the inside of the mitt about 2" (5cm), then bend it back to the raw edge. Pin in place. Fold the mitt pieces back together (right sides still together and loop sandwiched between them) and pin. Continue sewing the mitt together from the thumb down, catching the ends of the loop in the seam at the end, and backstitching back and forth over the loop. Trim off extra tape.

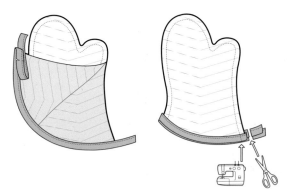

7. Finish the edges by zigzag stitching around the entire pot holder in the seam allowance, stopping at the thumb joint, then starting again around the thumb and down the other side. Clip the seam allowance at the thumb joint to ease the seam, and trim the seam allowance near the zigzag stitching to neaten the edges.

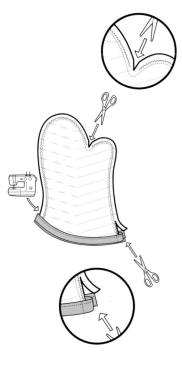

8. Turn the pot holder right side out, pushing out the thumb and top of mitt.

making your own bias tape

· ·

Although there are a few different ways to make your own bias tape, in most cases, simply cutting strips on the bias and sewing them together one by one will do the trick. Here are some basic instructions to make a few yards (2–3m) of your own ½" (13mm) double-fold bias tape:

1. You can begin with any amount of fabric, but starting with at least ½ yard (45.5cm) of material will give you nice long strips to work with, which speeds up the process. Beginning with your fabric face down, fold it on the bias by taking one of the selvage edges and lining it up with one of the cut edges, folding the fabric on a 45-degree angle. (The folded fabric will be shaped like a triangle.) Press along the folded edge. Now open up the fabric, and using the diagonal creased line as your guide, start drawing 2" (5cm) strips across the width of the fabric. Use a pencil to mark your lines.

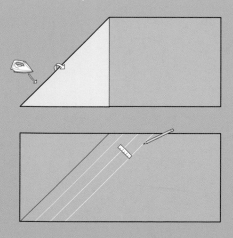

2. Cut the strips along the lines and sew them together: Place the strips right sides together, matching up the top angled raw edges. (Your strips will form an upside down V.) Sew the strips together at this edge using a ¼" (6mm) seam allowance. Continue adding strips together in this way. When your bias tape reaches the desired length, press the seam allowances open flat and trim any small "tails" of fabric from the seam ends.

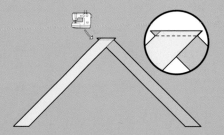

3. Folding the tape: Fold the long strip in half lengthwise with wrong sides together and press. Using this long center fold as your guide, fold the raw side edges in toward the center crease and press again. A bias-tape-making tool, such as the Clover Bias Tape Maker, works well for this.

4. Fold the tape in half again to enclose the raw edges and finish your tape. Press.

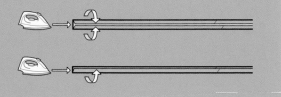

2

pretty presents
gifts for her

Mothers, sisters, daughters, girlfriends—what would we do without the women in our lives? So when it's time to celebrate one of your favorite gals, give her something as special as she is, made especially for her.

The gifts in this chapter can be given to women of all ages, shapes, and sizes. For example, the fabric bracelets on page 40 can take on a variety of looks depending on the fabric you choose. And almost every woman I know would like the cozy slippers on page 37. They're made from cheery, cherry dishtowels and will keep toes warm and smiles bright.

If you're looking to give just a little something (and you want a cute way to wrap it), check out the fabric-covered soaps on page 36. They're a super-easy way to dress up an ordinary item and turn it into a personalized token of affection. Finally, I hope you'll also make a few of these gifts for yourself. After making all these projects, you'll have earned it, girlfriend!

No-Sew Ribbon Belt

finished measurements
1½" x 44" (3.8cm x 112cm)

supplies

- Approximately 1½ yards (1.4m) of 1½"- (3.8cm-) wide ribbon

- Contrasting duct tape

- Scissors (or rotary cutter and self-healing mat)

- Plastic or acrylic belt buckle without a prong, and with an opening of 1½" or slightly wider.

- Double-sided tape

This super-easy belt is a knockoff of the popular Hadley Pollet ribbon belts that sell in stores for more than $100. This no-sew version, however, costs less than $15 and takes about half an hour to make. The secret: duct tape! The belt is lined with contrasting tape on the back, which gives it structure and allows you to fasten the buckle without requiring any sewing. You can use any width ribbon for this project—you'll just have to trim your duct tape to match. The belt makes a terrific last-minute birthday gift, and it's so easy you might want to whip up a few extras while you're at it. Go ahead—these belts are a cinch!

1. Measure your ribbon: When making this belt for others, measure around your own hips, then adjust accordingly. Measure around the hips where your belt loops are, then add an extra 11" (28cm). For example, if your hip measurement is 38" (96.5cm), you'll need to cut a 49" (124.5cm) length of ribbon. Cut the ribbon to the determined length.

2. Measure out a length of duct tape that is just a little longer than your ribbon. If your duct tape is *wider* than your ribbon, trim it to be just a tiny bit narrower than the ribbon. A rotary cutter and mat work well for this.

3. Cover the back of your ribbon with the strip of duct tape, then trim the ends of the taped ribbon so they are nice and clean.

4. Add the buckle: Loop the taped ribbon through the buckle, and "hem" back 2" (5cm) of it on the wrong side of the belt. Secure the hem on the inside using a couple small strips of

double-sided tape. "Hem" the other end of the belt by folding back 3" (7.5cm) of the taped ribbon, and again secure with double-sided tape.

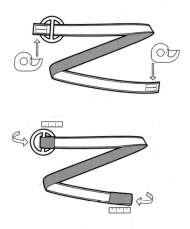

5. Cut another strip of duct tape, 3" (7.5cm) shorter in length than the belt, and trim the tape width if needed. Add this second strip of tape to the back of the belt, covering the first strip and the raw edges of the hems.

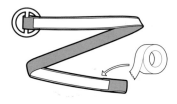

Celebrate making a cute, inexpensive present in less than 30 minutes!

all wrapped up

• • • • • • • • • •

Sometimes the way a gift is wrapped is as much a part of the present as the present itself! In this case, inexpensive soaps are elevated to elegant, one-of-a-kind gifts when wrapped in beautiful fabrics and tied with personalized tags. The challenge here was to get the material nice and crisp so it would be easy to fold. The solution: spray starch. The fabrics were starched and ironed several times then cleanly cut into rectangles just large enough to fold around the soap. The soaps were then wrapped like presents, tucking double-sided tape inside the flap edges to invisibly secure the fabric. These gifts are so pretty, they may *never* get unwrapped.

Dishtowel Slippers

Dishtowel Slippers

finished measurements

5" x 10½" (12.5cm x 26.5cm), about a women's shoe size 6–8

supplies

- Slipper pattern templates (page 122)
- 2 matching or complementary dishtowels
- 11½" x 24" (29cm x 61cm) piece gripper fabric for soles, such as Jiffy Grip (Resources, page 118)
- ¼ yard (23cm) craft batting (¼" [6mm] loft)
- ¼ yard (23cm) of 1"- (2.5cm-) thick foam
- Sewing machine
- Thread
- Iron and ironing board

Have you ever found yourself mesmerized by the beautiful patterns on dishtowels? I, for one, would rather use them for just about anything other than drying dishes! So why not fancy them up into something else—like a pair of cozy slippers? Dishtowels happen to be very soft and absorbent, making them the perfect material to snuggle up in after a shower or on a cold morning. The towels I used had a waffle weave, which reminded me of the slippers you might find at a fancy spa.

1. Photocopy the slipper pattern templates at the recommended percentage, and cut out the paper patterns. Use the patterns to cut out the following pieces, which will make both slippers:

   From the dishtowels:

   2 toe fronts, 2 toe linings, 2 top soles

   From the gripper fabric:

   2 bottom soles

   From the batting: 2 toe fronts

   From the foam: 2 foam inserts

   Note: The directions from this point on are for making one slipper at a time.

2. Pin the batting toe front to the wrong side of the toe lining, matching

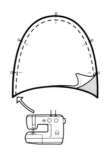

up the raw edges. Baste together using a ⅜" (9mm) seam allowance.

3. With right sides together, pin the dishtowel toe front to the toe lining, and stitch together along the bottom edge using a ½" (13mm) seam allowance. Clip the curves, turn pieces right side out, and press.

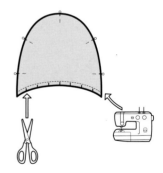

4. Trim the extra tails of fabric at the bottom side edges. Then baste together the toe front and lining pieces using a ⅜" (9mm) seam allowance. Use a pencil to mark the top center point of the toe in the seam

allowance. Then mark points 5" (12.5cm) up from each bottom corner. To ease the outer edge at the top of the toe, ease-stitch between these last 2 points by stitching along the seam line and then again ¼" (6mm) from the edge using a long machine stitch. Pull the threads to gather the fabric at the top of the toe.

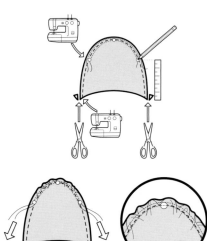

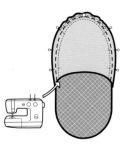

5. Mark the center top point of the bottom gripper sole. With right sides together and center points aligned, pin the right side of the toe to the right side of the bottom gripper sole. Sew together using a ½" (13mm) seam allowance.

6. With *right* sides together, lay sole top piece directly over the gripper sole bottom and toe. Pin, then sew together using a ½" (13mm) seam allowance. *Leave an opening at the top of the toe area.*

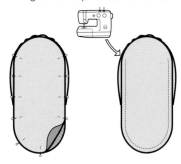

7. Turn the slipper inside out. Note that at this point the toe piece will be lining-side up.

8. Stuff the foam insert into the slipper through the opening at the toe.

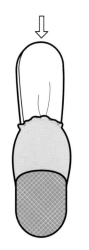

9. Pin and sew the top of the toe closed using a ½" (13mm) seam allowance, backstitching at the beginning and end of the seam and sewing through all layers of fabric.

Zigzag stitch along the raw edge to finish the seam.

10. Once the toe has been sewn closed, flip the toe section over. The toe section will now be right side out on the front of the slipper.

11. Repeat steps 2–10 to make the second slipper.

Fabric Bangles

LEVEL 2

finished measurements
3¼" (8.5cm) diameter

supplies (for 1 bangle)
- 1' (30.5cm) of ⁵⁄₁₆"- (8mm-) wide nylon-covered cotton rope (choose a light-colored rope with a smooth texture)
- Masking tape
- ¼ yard (23cm) fabric
- Cutting board
- Craft knife
- Iron and ironing board
- Straightedge
- Sewing machine and matching thread
- Long wooden skewer or chopstick
- Hand-sewing needle

Thanks!

These pretty bracelets are actually just fabric-covered rope, and they're one of my favorite gifts to give. I've made them for birthday and Mother's Day presents, and they can be dressed up or down depending on the fabric you choose.

I used ⁵⁄₁₆"- (8mm-) wide nylon-covered cotton rope from the hardware store for these bangles, but you can use smooth rope of any thickness—just adjust the width of the fabric accordingly. The rope is slipped into a presewn tube of fabric and then bent into a bracelet shape. The main trick with these bangles is to cut the fabric on the bias, allowing the material to stretch around the curved rope with hardly any gaps. You'll want to make an armful of these!

1. When making this bracelet for others, measure around your own wrist, allowing room for the bracelet to slide over your hand, then adjust accordingly. The bracelets pictured here are made with 9" (23cm) lengths of rope.

2. Tightly wrap the section where you plan to cut the rope with a piece of masking tape. This will help keep the cut edges from fraying. Using a cutting board and craft knife, cut the rope cleanly on both ends.

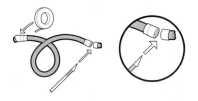

3. Fold your fabric on the bias by taking one of the selvage edges and lining it up with one of the cut edges so the fold is at a 45-degree angle. (The folded fabric will be shaped like a triangle.) With the fabric folded, measure over 1" (2.5cm) from the fold, and cut a strip about 12" (30.5cm) long using a straightedge. (Your strip will be 2" [5cm] wide when you open it.) If your rope is thicker or thinner than ⁵⁄₁₆" (8mm), add or subtract the difference to the 1" (2.5cm) folded strip.

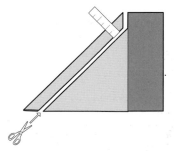

Open the strip flat and trim it to be 1" (2.5cm) longer than the rope.

(For example, for a 9" [21.5cm] rope, cut fabric strip to be 10" [25.5cm] long.)

4. With the fabric strip wrong side up, fold over ½" (13mm) on one of the long ends. Press.

5. Fold the fabric in half lengthwise, with *right* sides together. Pin in place, then stitch the long raw edges together using a ⅜" (9mm) seam allowance, backstitching at the beginning and end. Leave both ends open.

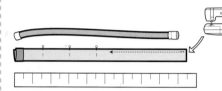

6. Starting at the hemmed end, and using a chopstick or wooden skewer to help, turn fabric right side out. Gently press.

7. Use the skewer to push the raw end inside the tube to give this end a ½" (13mm) "hem."

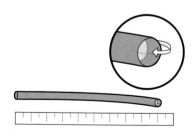

8. Starting at the end you just turned under, insert the rope into the fabric tube, pushing it through so it is completely covered by fabric. Adjust the folded raw edge if you need a tiny bit more or less fabric to cover the rope. Use the skewer at both ends to adjust the folded fabric to lie nice and flat against the rope.

9. Scrunch the fabric back to reveal the cut ends of the rope. Bend the rope into a bracelet shape, matching up the rope ends so they are tight and flush against each other. Tightly wrap a piece of masking tape around the seam to hold the rope ends together.

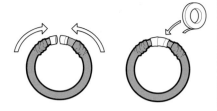

10. Scoot the fabric around to cover the taped seam. Then pull the fabric tight and line up the hemmed ends. Blind stitch the fabric tube closed at the ends using a needle and thread. Tie a knot and trim any threads.

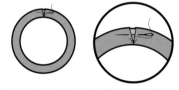

Washcloth Bag

Washcloth Bag

finished measurements
3" x 8½" x 5½" (7.5cm x 21.5cm x 14cm)

supplies
- 1 large washcloth, approximately 13" x 13" (33cm x 33cm)
- 1 roll of duct tape (in complementary color)
- Masking tape
- Stapler and staples
- Two ⅜" (9mm) grommets
- Grommet tool (or grommet pliers)
- Thin cotton cord or shoelace, approximately 22" (56cm) long
- White glue (optional)

How cute are washcloths? Plain white terry versions have taken a back seat to polka dots, stripes, zigzags, and just about any other pattern you can imagine. Easy to find (and often on sale), washcloths are the perfect material to use when you're looking for a sewing shortcut—the small dimensions and hemmed edges mean that most of the sewing is already done for you!

In fact, this little bag isn't sewn at all. The washcloth is lined with duct tape, which helps give it shape and makes the inside waterproof, and then the sides and bottom are stapled together instead of sewn. You can throw this cosmetic case together in about thirty minutes with materials you have lying around the house, making it a perfect last minute gift.

1. Open the washcloth wrong side up on a hard, flat surface. Cut off any tags.

2. Smooth out the washcloth and cover it with strips of duct tape, placed horizontally and overlapping slightly, until the entire washcloth has been lined. Place the first and last pieces of tape close to but not completely covering the top and bottom edges.

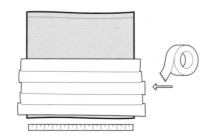

3. Trim the tape around the washcloth edges to neaten the sides and trim the taped washcloth down one side so it measures 9½" wide (24cm).

Note: Do not use your good fabric scissors when cutting the tape. Refer to Sticky Situation, opposite, for more information about cutting duct tape.

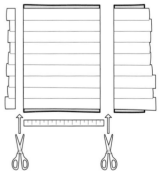

4. With right sides together, fold the fabric in half, lining up the top and bottom edges, to form a folded rectangle approximately 9½" (24cm) wide x 6½" (16.5cm) tall.

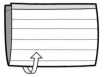

Use a couple pieces of masking tape to hold the folded material in place. Staple the sides together using a ½" (13mm) seam allowance, then cover the stapled seams with duct tape folded lengthwise over the raw edge. (You may want to make the tape narrower by tearing it down to 1" [2.5cm].) Trim off extra tape.

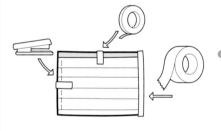

sticky situation

• • • • • • • • • • •

Cutting duct tape can be a real mess—and can really mess up your scissors. So if possible, designate a pair of craft scissors as your "tape scissors." Just wrap a little piece of masking tape around the handle to differentiate them from your good fabric shears. Keep your scissors goo-free by cleaning them with a little vegetable oil, then soap and water. Use several layers of paper towel to wipe the blades clean and to protect yourself from the scissors' sharp edges.

If you really want to cut tape without a hitch, invest in a pair of Teflon Scissors (Resources, page 118). As a devoted crafter once told me, cutting tape with Teflon scissors is "like butter!"

5. Make the bottom: With the bag still inside out, flatten one bottom corner to create a triangular point. Draw a 3" (7.5cm) line perpendicular to the side seam and 1½" (3.8cm) from the corner point. Staple along the line. If the washcloth material is really thick, you may need to turn the bag over and restaple the corner on the back as well. Repeat on the other bottom corner of the bag. Cover the staples with a narrow strip of duct tape folded over the side edges.

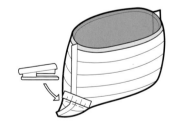

6. Add the grommets: Turn the bag right side out. Center the grommets on the top front and back of the bag, approximately 1" (2.5cm) from the top edge. Add grommets according to the package instructions.

7. Dab each end of the cotton cord with glue to stop it from unraveling. Let dry, then lace the cord through the grommets and tie to close the bag.

Pillowcase Tote

LEVEL 3

finished measurements
18 ¾" x 26" (47.5cm x 66cm)

supplies

- Standard pillowcase (approximately 20" x 30" [51cm x 76cm])

- Iron and ironing board

- Ruler

- Seam ripper

- 2 packages (8 yards) [7.3m] ¼"- (6mm-) wide double-fold bias tape in contrasting color

- Sewing machine and thread to match pillowcase and bias tape

I love shortcuts, especially when the end result looks anything but quick and easy! Because this reusable shopping tote is made from a pillowcase, it's halfway finished before you even start it. Using a standard pillowcase allows you to skip some of the cutting and sewing steps you'd normally encounter—which means less time fussing and more time creating! The bag is surprisingly strong and takes up almost no space when folded, making it a great shopping bag or extra travel tote.

1. Iron the pillowcase to get out all the wrinkles. Fold the pillowcase in half lengthwise with the opening at the top and the fold on the right. On the folded side edge, mark a point approximately 15" (38cm) from the bottom. On the opposite side, mark a point approximately 16" (40.5cm) from the bottom. On the top edges mark points approximately 3⅞" (10cm) in from each side. Draw the bag handles as shown, connecting each side point to the top of the pillowcase. Use a ruler to help draw straight lines and to keep the straps 2¼" (5.5cm) wide for the most part, until they begin to curve toward the side edges. Open the pillowcase up; it will look like a tank top.

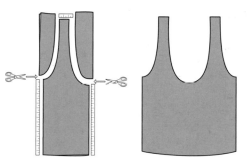

2. Using a seam ripper, rip out the pillowcase hem at the top of all the straps and iron flat.

3. Fold the pillowcase in half again, as before, and trim straps so the whole piece measures approximately 29" (74cm) from the bottom of the pillowcase.

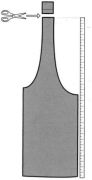

4. Open the pillowcase up again. Pin the two front straps to each other, right sides together, lining up the top raw edges (be sure to join the 2 front straps, *not* a front strap and a back strap). Sew the straps together using a wide 1¼" (3cm) seam allowance. Iron the seam open, then turn under each raw edge ½" (13mm) and iron again.

Attach the back straps to each other in the same manner.

5. Finish all raw edges with bias tape: Beginning on the front, cut a piece of bias tape long enough to go completely around the inside "armhole," cutting a few inches (5–8cm) more than you need. Open up the folded bias tape so the smaller of the folded sides is opened flat. Finish the first cut edge by folding over ½" (13mm) toward the *wrong* side of the binding. Press. Then, with right sides together, line up the raw edge of the side you just opened with the raw edge of the armhole, starting the tape a few inches (5–8cm) down from the strap seam you just sewed. Pin in place. Baste the bias tape to the front of the bag by sewing along the creased line (approximately a ¼" [6mm] seam allowance).

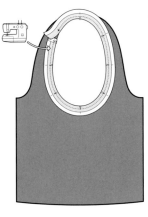

Fold the bias tape back over the raw edge of the fabric and pin in place.

Topstitch the bias tape on the front of the bag, close to the edge where the folded bias tape meets the pillowcase fabric.

Apply bias tape to the remaining "armhole" and then to the top raw edges in the same manner.

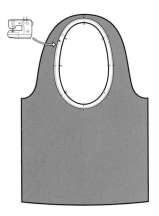

6. Make the bottom: Turn the bag inside out. Flatten one bottom corner to create a triangular point. Draw a 4" (10cm) line perpendicular to the side seam and 2" (5cm) from the corner point. Sew across this line, backstitching at each end. Then sew a second seam just below the first seam to reinforce the bottom of the bag. Turn the bag right side out.

rediscovering bias tape

I haven't spent a lot of time thinking about bias tape since I first used it to bind the edges of a smock in seventh-grade home ec. Bias tape was one of the sewing terms we had to define on the final exam, and we couldn't pass the class without providing a sample of the trim neatly applied. Recently, I uncovered a bunch of this wonder trim in the bottom of my sewing box and have had fun using it again. (In addition to the tote featured here, check out the bias-tape-trimmed Hot Stuff Pot Holder and Oven Mitt on page 26). The beauty of bias tape, as I was quickly reminded, is its "bend-ability." Because it's cut on the bias, or on a diagonal, it has more stretch and give than fabric cut on the straight of grain, so it can easily bend around corners and curves without any gaps or puckers.

Although it's not clear exactly when commercial bias tape began to be sold, there is evidence that it dates back to the late 1800s. Women often added a wide version of it to their floor-length skirts to protect them from the wear and tear of unpaved streets. By the twentieth century, store-bought tape had become extremely popular and was available in a huge variety of fabrics and colors. Hailed as the great sewing room labor saver, home sewers (of which there were many) used it as a quick, neat way to finish everything from aprons to negligees.

Today's prepackaged bias tapes are often made out of a poly-cotton blend, usually only in solid colors. But there's no need to settle for what you can find in the notions department. You can hunt down interesting old varieties on eBay, or easily make your own bias tape from favorite fabrics (Making Your Own Bias Tape, page 31).

3

it's a guy thing
gifts for him

When it comes to finding the perfect gifts, men can be particularly challenging. I've given my father more golf shirts than I care to admit, and my husband hasn't faired much better. But on a few occasions, I have come up with some guy gifts that have been home runs. For example, the photo baseball project on page 56 is always a hit. After all, what guy doesn't love tossing a ball around? And this one is personalized with favorite photos.

Many of the projects in this chapter are made from recycled or repurposed materials, like the Wonder Wallet (page 60) made from recycled comic-book pages, and Tailor-Made Frames (page 52), which utilize worn out men's dress shirts. Unlike a dress shirt, the wallet and frames are sure to fit. The rest of the projects in this chapter are also size neutral, making them great options for any guy on your gift list.

Tailor-Made Frames

finished measurements
small frames—5½" x 7⅜" x ⅝"
(14cm x 18.5cm x 15mm); larger
frame—9¼" x 7¼" x ½" (23.5cm x
18.5cm x 13mm)

supplies

- Wooden picture frame with a
  removable back

- Dress shirt

- ¾"- (2cm-) wide double-sided
  tape

- Pencil

- Ruler

- Small, sharp scissors

- All-purpose glue, such as Elmer's
  Glue

- Wooden skewer or chopstick

- Craft knife

- Computer with inkjet printer
  and 1 printable fabric sheet
  (often used for quilting)
  (for tags)

- Photograph to place in your
  frame

I hate to throw things out, as one look in my attic or basement will reveal! So when my husband was ready to retire a stack of dress shirts recently, I decided to snatch them up. The shirts were all damaged in some way: Frayed collars, ink spots, and a smattering of holes had done them in. But much of the fabric was still crisp and in good shape. You can make so many things out of recycled shirting fabric, but I wanted to come up with a gift item, ideally one that could be personalized. I decided to cover a store-bought frame with the fabric and made custom labels to give the frames a special shirtlike touch.

1. Remove the back and glass from your frame so you are working just with the wooden front part. Place the frame on the shirt and cut out around the frame, adding several extra inches (5–10cm) all around. Then, neatly cut the fabric into a rectangle large enough to fold up over the sides and back of the frame, plus an extra ½" (13mm) or so all around.

    Mark the inside frame corners on the fabric with a pencil, then connect the points with diagonal lines.

    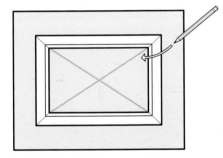

2. Place a few strips of double-sided tape on the front of the frame, then turn it over and center it face down on the wrong side of the fabric.

    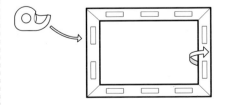

3. Cut on the lines with a pair of sharp scissors to create 4 flaps. (You may want to cut out a small rectangle in the center first to facilitate cutting.)

    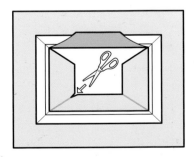

4. Glue the fabric flaps to the inside border of the frame (where the glass sits) one at a time. Use a wooden skewer to help pull fabric tight, then use a craft knife to cut away extra fabric. Repeat on all the sides.

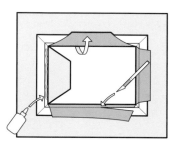

5. Cut the remaining fabric on a diagonal from the outer corners to the corner edges of the frame.

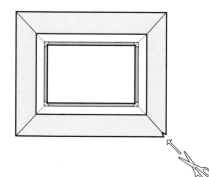

6. Fold the corners of the fabric back, toward the wrong side of the fabric, to form triangles at each corner of the fabric. Trim the folded corner pieces and side edges so the fabric neatly reaches

over and covers the back of the frame. Generously and evenly spread glue on the back of the frame and adhere the remaining fabric to the frame. The glue may seep through the fabric as it dries.

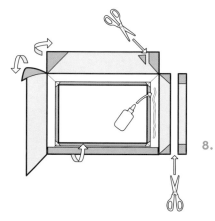

7. Make the tag (optional): Use your computer to design a tag for the frame. Print the tag on a printable fabric sheet using an inkjet printer. Trim the tag, and add stitching if desired. Attach the tag to the frame using a thin layer of glue or a piece of double-sided tape. Refer to Making Personalized Tags, page 64, for more information on tags.

8. Assemble the frame, inserting a photograph of your choice.

DIY printable fabric sheets

· · · · · · · · · · · · · · · · · · · ·

Making your own printable fabric sheets is fun and surprisingly easy. You'll need just a few supplies:

- ¼ yard (23cm) light- or medium-weight 100% cotton fabric (such as broadcloth or lightweight canvas)
- Iron and ironing board
- Scissors (or rotary cutter, straightedge, and self-healing mat)
- Freezer paper or full-sheet adhesive labels
- Lint roller (optional)

1. Iron the fabric to get out all the wrinkles.

2. Cut the fabric into a 9½" x 12" (24cm x 30.5cm) rectangle.

3. Attach the backing to the fabric, using either freezer paper or a full-sheet adhesive label in the following manner:

If using freezer paper: Place the fabric wrong side up on a smooth, cloth-covered heat-resistant surface, such as a formica table, counter, or wood shelf. (You can also work on an ironing board, but sometimes you will get a better bond if you iron on a harder surface.) Cut an 8½" x 11" (21.5cm x 28cm) piece of freezer paper, and center it, shiny side down, on top of the fabric. Iron the paper to the fabric using a dry iron on the cotton setting until the paper adheres.

Turn over, and iron again on the fabric side to make it nice and smooth.

If using an adhesive label: Place the fabric wrong side up on a smooth work surface or ironing board. Peel the backing off of the label, and center the label, sticky side down, onto the fabric. Use a cool iron to smooth the label and to remove any air bubbles.

4. Trim away extra fabric so it is flush with the backing. (A rotary cutter, straightedge, and mat work well for this.) Cut all loose threads, and use a lint roller to clean up any pieces of fuzz from the fabric.

5. Your fabric sheet is now ready to be fed through an inkjet printer. Make sure to load your fabric sheets properly, so you are printing on the fabric side.

Life's a Ball! Photo Baseball

finished measurements

9¼" (23.5cm) in circumference

supplies

- Baseball pattern template (page 123)

- Photos

- Computer with scanner and inkjet printer

- 1 T-shirt transfer sheet

- Iron and ironing board

- 2 T-shirts, one white, one colored

- Scotch matte-finish "Magic" tape or clear cellophane tape

- Sewing machine and matching thread

- 1 regulation-size baseball, preferably a rubber "practice" baseball

- Red embroidery floss and needle (optional)

It took me several tries and a lot of patience before I figured out how to make this photo baseball look and feel like the real thing. I finally realized the best thing to do was to cover an actual baseball! A soft rubber "practice" baseball worked best because of its smooth outer texture, but an official leather ball works too. A combination of hand- and machine-sewing gets the fabric cover to fit nice and snug. I also decided to cover only one panel with photos, which are applied using a T-shirt transfer. The other panel is made from plain, stretchy T-shirt material, which allows you to easily pull the fabric cover over the ball.

This makes a special gift for any guy, but grandpas, dads, and baseball-obsessed sons (like mine) are especially happy to receive it. For a fun gift-wrapping idea, check out the Baseball-Card Wrapping Paper on page 59.

1. Photocopy the baseball template at the recommended percentage and carefully cut out the pattern, keeping the outer frame of paper around the template mostly intact. You will use this paper silhouette to help you "frame up" your photos. Place your photos under the cutout opening and arrange them so they fit within the border. Remember that you will lose a ¼" (6mm) all around for the seam allowance when you sew your ball cover together.

2. Carefully move the photos to the scanner. Scan the photos, then print out the scan on a scrap of paper to recheck the photo placement.

stitched in time

• • • • • • • • • •

Did you know that baseballs (every one that has real stitching on it) are all sewn by hand? Although machines make the inside of the balls, there is no machine to sew on the baseball cover. It takes about eight minutes to hand stitch a baseball, which is longer than the average lifespan of a major-league ball: four to seven pitches.

When you are happy with the lay-out, print the image on photo transfer paper.

Note: Select the mirror-image option when you print, otherwise the photos will be flipped when you iron them. If you don't have a scanner, use a piece of tape to hold the photos in place and have a copy store print your transfer.

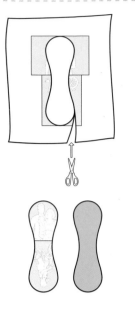

3. Iron your transfer onto a piece of white T-shirt material following the package instructions.

4. Using a few pieces of tape to hold the baseball pattern template in place, cut out a baseball piece from the photo fabric. Use the template again to cut out a second baseball piece out of the colored fabric.

5. Fold the baseball piece with photos on it in half lengthwise and mark the center top with a pencil or pin. Fold the contrast-ing fabric piece in half width-wise and mark the center spot with a pencil or pin.

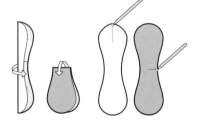

With right sides together, line up the center dots and the raw edges, and begin hand-basting the 2 pieces together using a scant ⅛" (3mm) seam allowance. Con-tinue all the way around, carefully matching up raw edges, leaving about 4½" (11.5cm) open at the end. Knot and cut thread.

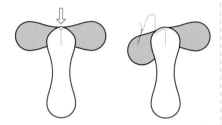

6. Once pieces are hand-basted to-gether, stitch them again on the machine using a ¼" (6mm) seam allowance. Stitch on the con-trasting T-shirt side, carefully turning the material as you round the curves.

baseball stitch how-to

· · · · · · · · · · · · · · · · ·

The baseball stitch is a decorative stitch used to join two fabric edges that abut each other. Begin by inserting your needle in the "ditch" where the two edges meet, and then bring it back out on one of the pieces of fabric, a little more than ⅛" (3mm) from the edge. Then poke your needle back down through the "ditch" again, and bring it back out on the opposite piece of fabric, again a little more than ⅛" (3mm) from the edge. Continue stitching like this, angling your stitches slightly if desired, to mimic the stitching on a real baseball.

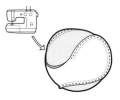

Trim the seam allowances to ⅛" (3mm) (leaving the full ¼" [6mm] at the opening), then turn the cover right side out.

7. Slip the ball into the cover. Pull the photo fabric tight around the ball, smoothing out wrinkles, and hold the fabric in place by sticking it to the ball with straight pins. Adjust the fabric placement as necessary, tucking under a ¼" (6mm) seam allowance on the colored piece of fabric, and repin just on top of the photo fabric.

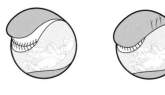

8. Carefully blind-stitch the seam closed.

9. If desired, add "baseball" stitching to the seams using red embroidery floss.

baseball-card wrapping paper

Scan or color-copy rows of baseball cards to make your own one-of-a-kind wrapping paper. The sheets are perfect for wrapping any gift, especially baseball themed presents. Use extra long, colorful rubber bands to tie things up—just like a stack of baseball cards!

Refer to Baseball Stitch How-To, opposite, for more information on this type of stitch.

Wonder Wallet

finished measurements

8⅛" x 3⁵⁄₁₆" (20.6cm x 8.5cm)

supplies

- 1 standard comic book, (approximately 6⅝" x 10⅛" [17cm x 25.5cm])

- 1 package 17" x 2-yard (43cm x 1.8m) iron-on vinyl (Resources, page 118)

- Iron and ironing board

- Clear cellophane tape

- Sewing machine

- Thread

- Scissors (or a rotary cutter, straightedge, and self-healing mat)

- Coffee mug or can approximately 3¾" (8cm) in diameter

Guys of all ages (especially those who are young at heart!) will love this wallet made from laminated comic book pages. A layer of iron-on vinyl is all that is needed to turn the vibrant adventures and iconic images into sturdy, eye-catching fabric for this unique guy gift.

The wallet is made from three comic book pages (one 2-page spread taped to another single page), which are then folded together, sort of like an origami project. A row of machine stitches on each side edge finishes things up, and makes the wallet strong enough to withstand wear and tear from even the toughest superhero.

1. Take the staples out of the center of the comic book, so you can separate all the pages without tearing them.

2. Select three pages with which to make your "material," using one 2-page spread plus one additional single page. Turn the pages right side down, then use a strip of cellophane tape to connect the 2-page section to the single page, lining up the edges so they are flush. Trim off any extra tape. You will have made a rectangle that is approximately 20" wide x 10" tall (51cm x 25.5cm).

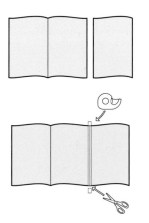

3. Now turn the material so it is vertical, with the 2-page spread section at the top.

   On the 2-page section only, beginning at the top, fold the material forward and back to make a 4-section accordion pleat.

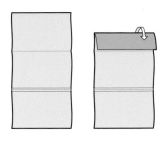

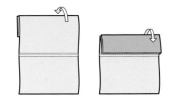

4. Open up the pleat. At the bottom end, fold up a 4" (10cm) flap. Then fold the accordion pleat back down. (It will cover part of the flap.)

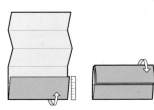

5. Fold this bottom section up to make a 2½" (6.5cm) flap as shown. Make sure all creases are crisp.

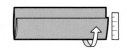

6. Fold the wallet in half widthwise and crease. Unfold the wallet, opening up the material completely. Laminate the right side of the material with iron-on vinyl, following package instructions. Afterward, fold the wallet back up as it was before, following the folds and creases.

7. Make a cutout for credit cards: Mark an X in the center of the inside flap.

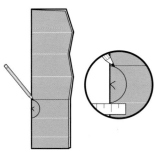

Open the material completely again, and fold it in half lengthwise. On the section where you've marked the X, use a curved edge, such as the bottom of a coffee mug, to draw an arc 1⅛" (3cm) from the fold. With material still folded, cut out the credit card opening.

8. Fold the wallet back up, following folds and creases. (If desired, you can laminate the paper section behind the credit card opening first.) Once the wallet is folded back up, stitch the side seams closed using a 1" (2.5cm) seam allowance, backstitching at the beginning and end. Trim extra fabric on each side close to the stitching, and trim all threads.

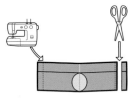

His (and Hers) Washroom Bag

finished measurements

4" x 9½" x 6" (10cm x 24cm x 15cm)

supplies

- 16" x 20" (40.5cm x 51cm) piece duck cotton or canvas

- "Men's Room" illustration (found at hardware stores or online)

- 1 sheet T-shirt transfer paper for dark fabrics

- Scotch matte-finish "Magic" tape

- Small sharp scissors

- 16" x 20" (40.5cm x 51cm) piece of iron-on vinyl (Resources, page 118)

- Iron and ironing board

- Parchment paper

- 24" (61cm) or longer heavyweight nylon coil zipper (sometimes referred to as an upholstery zipper)

- Sewing machine and matching thread

- 1' (30.5cm) of 1"- (2.5cm-) wide nylon webbing

- Duct tape to match canvas

- Computer with inkjet printer

- 1 printable fabric sheet (often used for quilting)

This canvas dopp kit is just the right size for business travel and just the right gift for the guy who's always on the go. It's decorated with an iron-on transfer of the classic "Men's Room" icon, which you can make yourself using T-shirt transfer paper designed especially for dark fabric. Of course, this "His" bag could just as easily be made for "Her"—or make one of each! The pair makes a great engagement or anniversary present.

1. Cut out the bag: Fold the fabric in half to form a 16" x 10" (40.5cm x 25.5cm) rectangle. Cut out a 3"- (7.5cm-) wide x 5½"- (14cm-) tall rectangle from each side, 2¼" (5.5cm) from the top edge and bottom fold as shown.

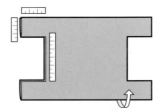

2. Make the decal: Size the men's room image on your computer or on a copy machine to be approximately 4" (10cm) tall. Roughly cut out the image from the printout and tape it directly to the back of a T-shirt transfer sheet made for dark material. (You will not be printing on the transfer sheet, as you normally would. Instead, you will cut the image out of the transfer paper, using

the printout as your guide.) Using small sharp scissors, carefully cut out the image. Peel away the backing paper. Position the image, face up, on the right side of the fabric, in the center of the folded material, as shown. Following the package instructions, iron the image in place.

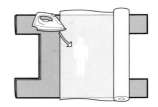

3. Apply iron-on vinyl: Cut out a piece of iron-on vinyl in the same shape as the canvas, following the instructions in step 1. Place the canvas fabric, wrong side up, on an ironing board. Place a piece of parchment paper in between your ironing board and the decal to protect it. Following the package instructions, iron the vinyl to the wrong side of the canvas, being careful not to iron too long over the area where the decal is on the other side.

4. Now that your fabric is finally prepared, it's time to start making the bag! Begin with the zipper: With the right side of the fabric facing the right side of the zipper, pin or tape the zipper to the top raw canvas edge (there will be a few inches [5–8cm] of extra zipper hanging off both sides). The zipper should be closed, and the zipper pull should be on the left side. Using a ¼" (6mm) seam

allowance, stitch the zipper to the canvas, guiding your regular presser foot against the zipper teeth as you go.

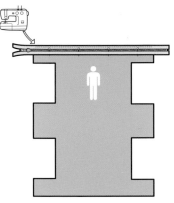

5. Finger-press the zipper back so it faces up. Topstitch close to the canvas edge to secure the zipper in place.

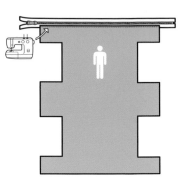

Repeat steps 4 and 5 to attach the zipper to the other side of the canvas.

6. Make the end tab: Cut a 2" (5cm) length of webbing. Fold it in half widthwise and place it on the left side of the bag. (This is where the zipper pull will end up when the bag is zipped closed.) Unzip the bag slightly, and center the tab over the zipper teeth on the left-hand side of the bag (with the bag fabric right side up), lining up the raw edges of the folded tab with the raw edge of the fabric. Baste in place using a ¼" (6mm) seam allowance.

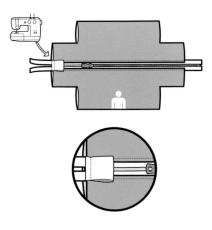

making personalized tags

. . . .

You can make your own personalized tags using your computer and printable fabric sheets for inkjet printers. Choose a font style you like, then design your tag, printing it out on paper first so you can finalize the dimensions. You can make your tag any size you want, but a good rule of thumb is to make a tag, when folded, ⅝" (15mm) taller than the seam allowance of the project. So if you are working with a ½" (13mm) seam allowance, you should design a tag that is 1⅛" (2.8mm) tall when folded in half (fold at the top). The writing, of course, should also be near the top of the tag, near the fold. This way, when you sew the tag in place (see individual pattern instructions), it will pop out and be little more than ½" (13mm) tall. The width of your tag will depend on the length of your text—just leave a little room on each side of the writing. After you've finalized your dimensions, print the tag out on a printable fabric sheet, and trim it to the desired size.

7. Sew up the zipper ends: Turn the bag inside out. (This is easier to do if you open the zipper up.) Then close the zipper again so it is mostly but not completely closed, and flatten the bag so the side edges line up. Stitch the ends closed using a ¼" (6mm) seam allowance, sewing back and forth a few times over the zipper. Trim off the extra zipper length at each end.

Note: Before stitching, make sure the zipper slider is on the inside *part of the bag.*

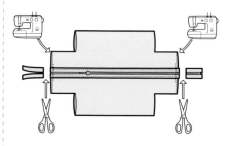

8. Cut a ¾" (2cm) strip of duct tape ½" (13mm) shorter than the sewn end. Center the tape on the seam so that it leaves some fabric exposed on both ends and fold the tape lengthwise to cover each seam, enclosing the zipper.

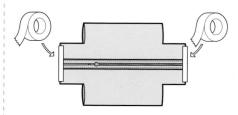

9. Make the tag: Use your computer to design a tag. Print the tag on a printable fabric sheet using an inkjet printer. Cut out the tag, fold it in half, and remove the backing paper before placing the tag in the bag. (The "his" and "hers" tags shown here are approximately 1" x ¾" [2.5cm x 2cm] after being trimmed and folded.) Refer to Making Personalized Tags, opposite, for more information.

10. Attach the tag and the strap: Cut a 5" (12.5cm) length of webbing to form the strap. With the writing going from top to bottom, baste the tag to the left end of the strap, matching up the raw ends.

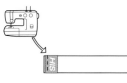

11. On the end of the bag without the end tab, position the strap inside the bag (which is still inside-out), centering the strap over the end seam.

When positioning the strap, make sure that the writing on the tag faces out (not toward the fabric), and that the tag is placed closest to the decal side of the bag. (This way, when the bag is turned right side out, the tag will pop out and be in the right place.) Baste the strap into place.

Pinch the open sides of the bag together, then pin them together. Stitch the sides closed using a ¼" (6mm) seam, sewing back and forth a few times over the strap to reinforce.

Repeat on the other end of the bag, but do not add a strap. Trim the loose threads and neaten up the edges.

Fold thin strips of duct tape lengthwise around all seams, then trim the tape to neaten the edges. Turn the bag right side out.

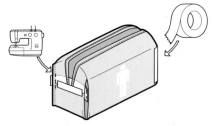

4

kiddin' around!
gifts for kids

Kids' presents are the perfect DIY projects. By nature, they are usually small in size and therefore require very little in terms of materials. And precisely because they *are* small, gifts for wee ones are so cute and so much fun to make! Creating things for kids also lets us tap into the childlike part of ourselves. Remember how satisfying it was to color, paint rocks, and cut and paste? Sewing and crafting are just grown up versions of activities like these, and making projects with kids in mind gives us an even greater opportunity to let down our hair, make a mess, and have fun.

For kids, anything and everything is a possible art supply—paper plates, Popsicle sticks, and of course, cardboard boxes. I still love finding ways to use ordinary objects to create new, beautiful things, and all the projects in this chapter incorporate easy-to-find materials from places like the supermarket and office supply store—even the recycling bin. My continuing love affair with cardboard boxes, for example, inspired the Take Note Journals on page 73, made from cereal, detergent, and candy boxes. And one of my favorite projects in the book is the pair of Shammy Jammies on page 68. These little baby lounging pajamas are made from super-soft cotton "shammy" dust cloths that I found at the grocery store. So before you start the projects in this chapter, give yourself permission to look at the world around you through a child's eye—it might help you discover "new" things that are right under your nose.

Shammy Jammies

finished measurements

top—21" x 10 5/8" (53.5cm x 27cm);
pants—11" x 15 1/2" (28cm x 39.5cm)

supplies

- Six to eight 16" x 22" (40.5cm x 56cm) cotton shammy cloths

- Iron and ironing board
- Shammy Jammies pattern templates (page 124)
- Sewing machine
- Yellow thread
- Pinking shears
- ½ yard (45.5cm) of ½"- (13mm-) wide elastic
- Two ⅜" (9mm) snaps
- Silk flower, such as a faux daisy (optional)
- Safety pin

To distract myself from the monotony of grocery shopping and the task of figuring out what to make for dinner, I sometimes look for hidden craft supplies at the supermarket. My treasure hunts have unearthed some great stuff, like the soft shammy dust cloths I used to make these cute baby lounging pajamas.

The bright yellow cloths were tucked away in a section of the store devoted to automotive supplies and housewares, and they were super soft and very inexpensive, but what really caught my eye was the bold red stitching that finished the edges—the perfect prefinished decorative trim. The jammies are just the right size for a six- to nine-month-old baby, and the yellow fabric makes them pretty gender neutral, though adding a little flower at the snap lends a "girlie" touch.

For top and pants. Iron the shammy cloths to get out all the wrinkles. Photocopy the templates at the recommended percentage and cut out all the pieces for the pajama top and pants before you begin.

For the front and back top pieces: Line up the bottom and side edges of the patterns with the finished, sewn edges on the shammy cloths as indicated on the template. (If possible, cut both top front pieces from one folded shammy cloth, and both top back pieces from another.)

For the front and back pants pieces: You will most likely need one shammy cloth for each pants piece. Place 2 cloths together, wrong sides facing, and line up the bottom edges of the patterns with the finished, sewn edges of the shammy cloths. Cut out the front pants pieces from one set of cloths, and the back pants pieces from another.

For the facing pieces: Cut out the facing pieces from the leftover material.

Pajama Top

1. With right sides together, pin the top back pieces together. Sew the back together along the long,

straight edge using a ½" (13mm) seam allowance. Trim the seam with pinking shears, then iron the seam open flat.

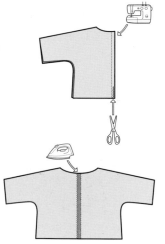

2. With right sides together, pin the top front pieces to the back. Sew together from the shoulder to the cuff and from the cuff to the bottom hem using a ½" (13mm) seam allowance. Clip the corners under the arms and trim the seam allowances with pinking shears. At the neck and sleeve openings, iron the seams flat.

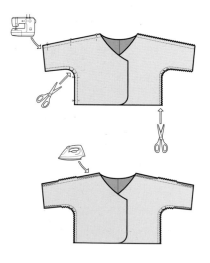

3. With right sides together, sew the front facings to the back facing at the shoulders using a ½" (13mm) seam allowance. Trim the seam allowances with pinking shears, and press flat. Trim the outer and bottom edges of the facing with pinking shears as well, but leave the inside edge as is.

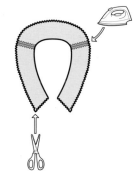

4. Turn the pajama top right side out and press. With right sides together, pin the facing to the neck, matching up the raw edges, then stitch together using a ½" (13mm) seam allowance. Clip curves and trim the seam allowances to ¼" (6mm) using regular scissors.

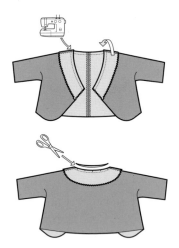

5. Turn the facing over and press to the inside. On the outside of the garment, stitch the facing down around the neck using a 1" (2.5cm) seam allowance.

6. Hem the sleeves: Trim the sleeve edges with pinking shears, then turn under a 1" (2.5cm) hem, and iron flat. Using a ¾" (2cm) seam allowance, and keeping the inside seams opened flat, sew down the hem.

Note: You will need to sew with your presser foot on the inside of the sleeve, backstitching at the beginning and end.

7. Add snaps: With the pajama top right side out, lay the right front over the left. Add snaps, placed as you desire, following the package instructions.

Pajama Pants

1. With right sides together, pin one front pants piece to one back pants piece and sew together along the inside leg edge using a ½" (13mm) seam allowance, backstitching at the beginning and end. Trim the seam allowance with pinking shears, then press the seam toward the back. Repeat with the remaining front and back pants pieces.

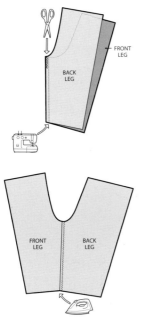

2. With right sides together, place both sets of front and back pieces together, matching up the inside leg seams and curved edges. Pin the leg sections together at the crotch, then stitch together using a ½" (13mm) seam allowance, backstitching at the beginning and end. Trim the seam allowance with pinking shears, then press the seam to one side. To help identify the back of the pants, place a safety pin at the center back seam as a marker.

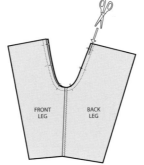

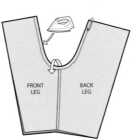

3. Prepare to sew outer side seams: To orient your fabric to sew up the sides, first turn the front and back pieces *right side* out.

Next, fold the raw edges toward each other, and pin the back of the pants to the front of the pants at the sides. Stitch the sides using a ½" (13mm) seam allowance, backstitching at the beginning and end. Trim the seam allowances with pinking shears, and press the seams toward the back. Remove safety pin.

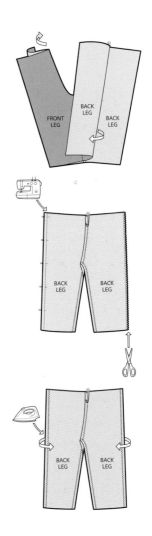

4. Form the waist casing: To form the waist casing, turn over 1½" (3.8cm) of fabric (toward the wrong side of the material) at the top of the pants. Press. Turn the raw edge under another ½"

(13mm), and press again. Stitch almost all the way around the waist, leaving an inch (2.5cm) or so opening at the back center of the waist to insert the elastic.

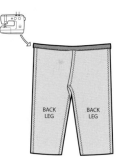

5. Cut elastic at a comfortable waist measurement plus 1" (2.5cm) (approximately 14 ½" [37cm] long). Use a safety pin attached at one end of the elastic to help thread the elastic through the casing. Stitch the ends of the elastic together, using a ½" (13mm) seam allowance and backstitching at the beginning and end.

flower power

· · · · · · · · · · · ·

To add a frilly touch to your jammies, place a flower in between the snap and the fabric before you attach your snaps. You can use a single layer from a silk flower or make your own flower from a piece of felt. If using a silk flower, first pull the entire flower off its plastic stem, then remove the green plastic "calyx"—the little base on the bottom—from the back of the flower. This will allow you to separate the flower into several different layers. By placing the thin layer in between the snap and the fabric, the flower will be held securely in place when the snap is set.

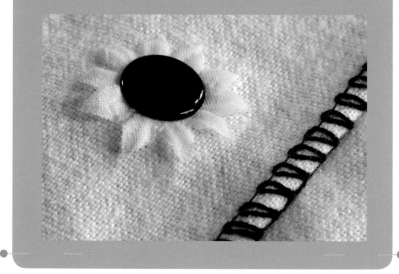

6. Stretch the elastic to allow the casing to lie flat, then stitch the casing closed.

Adjust the gathers around the waist so the pants fall nicely.

Take Note Journals

Take Note Journals

finished measurements (for journals shown)

Jujyfruits—4¾" x 6½" (12cm x 16.5cm);

Tide—7⅝" x 10" (19.5cm x 25.5cm);

Wheaties—5¼" x 7½" (13.5cm x 19cm)

supplies

- Empty cardboard boxes

- Rotary cutter or craft knife

- Straightedge

- Self-healing mat

- White poster board or plain, thin cardboard for the back cover (optional)

- Recycled filler paper or discarded printer paper

- Paper cutter (optional; you can have the copy store trim your filler paper, if desired)

- Plastic or metal spiral binding coil (you will need to get your book bound at a copy or print shop)

These recycled notebooks make great gifts for kids—that is, if you can wrestle them away from the adults who will want first dibs. When isolated, the colorful graphics from ordinary cardboard boxes look like pop art—thank you, Andy Warhol! After you decide on a design for the cover, fill the inside with recycled lined or graph paper, or use discarded printer paper (blank sides up!). These books are very easy to make and *very* addictive—you'll never throw out another cereal box again.

1. With the cardboard box open flat, isolate the image you want for the front of your notebook and cut it out of the box using a rotary cutter or craft knife. Make sure all sides are squared up. Since you are making your own notebook, it can be any size, with any number of pages. Some traditional notebook sizes include:

8" x 10½" (20.5cm x 26.5cm)

8½" x 11" (21.5cm x 28cm)

5" x 7" (12.5cm x 18cm)

3½" x 5" (9cm x 12.5cm)

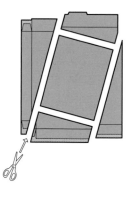

recycled gift tags

Use leftover scraps of cardboard to make these eye-catching recycled gift tags. They add a great punch of color and design to any package. Or make a bunch of them to give as a gift! Use a small manila shipping tag for your pattern, then cut out the tags from cardboard boxes with a rotary cutter or craft knife. Punch a hole and add a simple white reinforcement ring and a twine tie to make the tags look "official."

2. Use a leftover box scrap or a plain piece of cardboard or poster board to make the back of the notebook. Cut it the same size as the front.

3. Cut a stack of filler paper the same size as the cover. Use a paper cutter to make sure edges are even, or have the copy store cut the paper for you.

4. Bind your book at a copy store using a plastic or metal spiral binding.

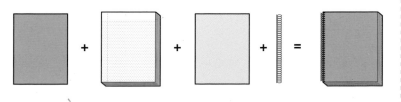

Nice to Meet You! Onesie

finished measurements
8½" x 15" (21.5cm x 38cm)

supplies
- "Hello, My Name Is" self-adhesive name badge
- Permanent marker
- Computer with scanner and inkjet printer
- 1 sheet T-shirt transfer paper for dark fabrics
- Cotton baby Onesie, 3–6 month size
- Iron and ironing board

Here's an easy way to turn a basic cotton Onesie into a unique gift that will help new parents introduce their little bundle to the world: Decorate it with an iron-on transfer of the classic "Hello, My Name Is" sticker. Just write the baby's name on the sticker first, then scan it and print it out using iron-on transfer paper made especially for dark T-shirts. (The transfer paper for dark material produces a "decal" that looks like a real name badge.) To make the girl's Onesie, I took a blue sticker to the copy store and had them adjust the levels on their color copy machine to produce a pink image.

Since this one-of-a-kind present can be made in less than an hour, keep a few blank Onesies on hand so you're always ready to welcome the newest newborn in style.

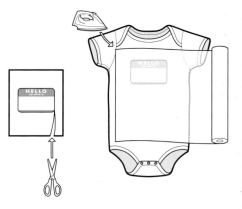

1. Write the baby's name on the sticker using a permanent marker, then scan it and print it out on the T-shirt transfer paper. (If you don't have a scanner, a copy store can copy and print out the image for you.)

2. Carefully cut around the image. Remove the backing paper and center the image face up on the top front of the Onesie. Apply the transfer according to package instructions.

3. Wrap up your personalized baby present, using a blank "Hello, My Name Is" sticker as your gift tag!

I'm Stuffed! Fabric Cans

finished measurements
soup—2½" x 3⅞" (6.5cm x 10cm);
tomatoes—4" x 4½" (10cm x
11.5cm)

supplies (for 1 can)

- Canned good with label

- Craft knife

- Computer with scanner and
  inkjet printer

- Printable fabric sheets for inkjet
  printer (often used for quilting)

- ¼ yard (23cm) silver heat-
  resistant ironing board fabric

- Needle and thread

- 1 yard (91cm) craft batting (¼"
  [6mm] loft) or 1"- (2.5cm-) thick
  foam plus a ¼ yard (23cm) craft
  batting

- Duct tape, any color

These "stuffed" food cans are a twist on ordinary children's building blocks, and they're a big hit with the two-to-five-year-old set! Kids love to play with "real" foods they recognize from Mom's kitchen, so why not make a soft, safe set of canned goods that are just the right size for little hands to hold? The can fabric is made by scanning real labels and printing them onto printable fabric sheets. Silvery heat-resistant ironing board fabric, available at most fabric stores, mimics the look of the tin tops. The cans are hand-sewn and surprisingly sturdy—perfect for cooking up lots of fun in busy little kitchens.

1. Carefully remove the label from the can by cutting along the seam with a craft knife. Scan the label and print it out on a scrap of paper first, adjusting it so it is slightly larger than actual size. (You want the label image to be as tall as the whole can, including the rim.) Cut out the sample label and check the size around the real can. The ends should overlap a little when you fold it around; just make sure the height of the label image is as tall as the whole can.

2. Once you've got the size you want, lay out the image on your computer with at least ½" (13mm) of extra room around the label. (For large cans, you may need to cut the image in half for it to fit on an 8½" x 11" (21.5cm x 28cm) piece of fabric transfer paper.) Print out the image, then cut out the label, adding an extra ⅛" (3mm) on the top and the bottom of the image, and ¼" (6mm) extra on each end. Follow package instructions to make fabric colorfast.

3. Cut out the top and bottom of the can: Make a pattern for the top and bottom by tracing around the can. Measure across the circle you've just traced, then draw a

new circle that is ¼" (6mm) bigger in diameter. Cut out 2 circles from the silver fabric using the new, enlarged circle as your pattern.

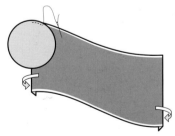

4. Assemble the pieces: Before sewing the pieces together, fold over the extra ¼" (6mm) on the ends of the label fabric, finger pressing the material toward the wrong side of the label. Then, with right sides together, begin sewing the top of the can to the label, carefully lining up the edges and hand-sewing the pieces together using a ⅛" (3mm) seam allowance.

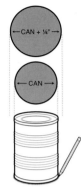

Repeat, sewing the bottom of the can to the bottom of the fabric label.

Turn the can right side out.

5. Make the stuffing: Measure the height of your can. Cut a long strip of batting or foam that is as wide as the can is tall. Roll the strip of material so that it is slightly smaller in diameter than the can. Tape the roll closed with a few strips of duct tape.

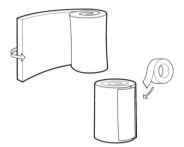

6. Place the stuffing inside the can and check the fit. Remove the roll, and add more batting if necessary for it to fit snugly inside the fabric can. Cut 2 circles out of batting, the same size as the finished top and bottom of the can, and place them inside the can at each end. Then add the roll of stuffing.

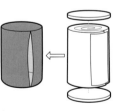

7. Blind stitch the sides closed using a needle and thread. Tie a knot and trim any loose threads.

Heartthrob Headband

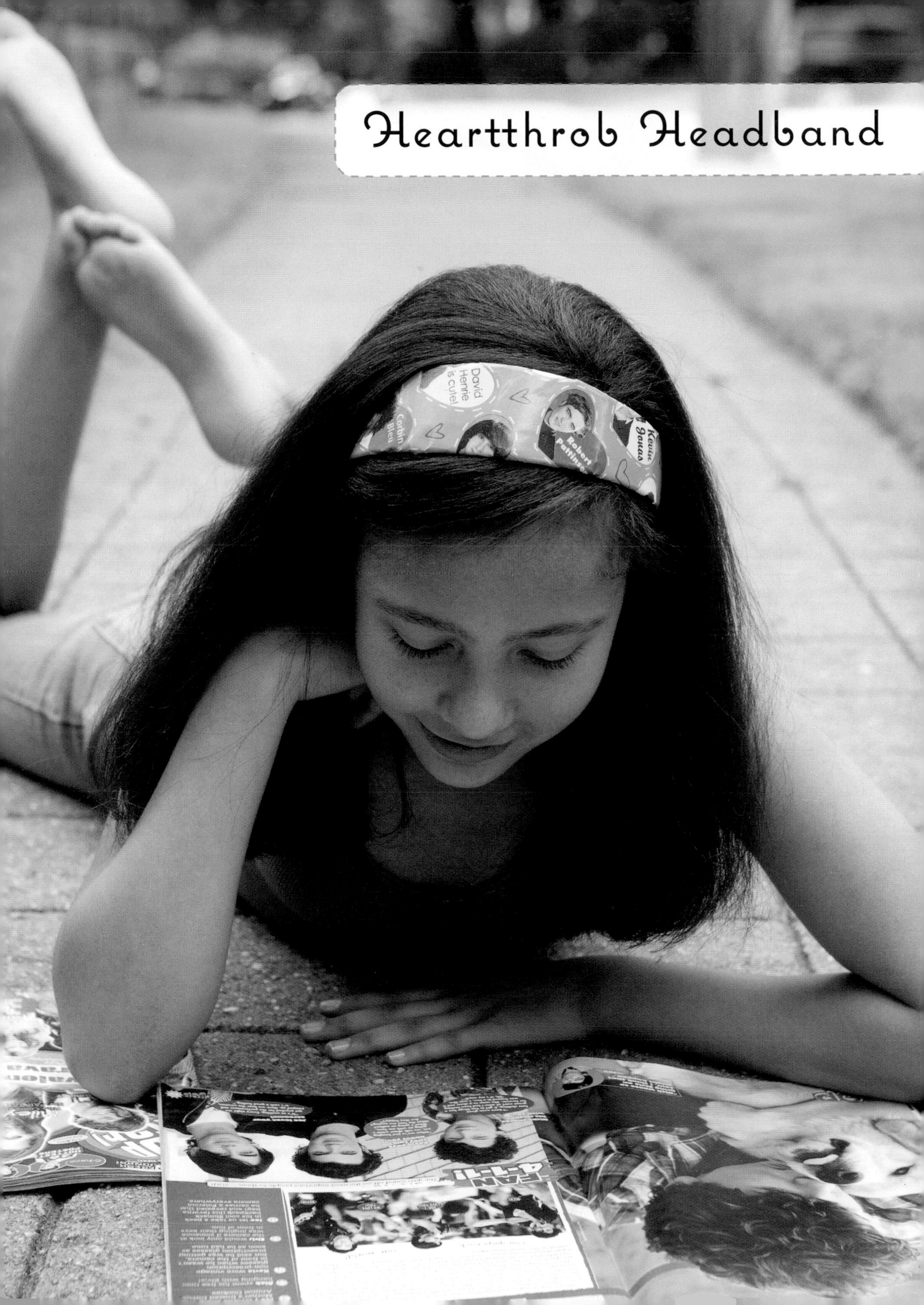

Heartthrob Headband

finished measurements

2" x 14¼" (5cm x 36cm)

supplies

- 2"- (5cm-) wide undecorated plastic headband without teeth (Resources, page 118)

- Teen magazine such as *Bop* or *Tiger Beat*

- 1 package 17" x 2-yard (43cm x 1.8m) iron-on vinyl (Resources, page 118)

- Iron and ironing board

- Clear cellophane tape or Scotch matte-finish "Magic" tape

- ½"- (13mm-) wide double-sided tape

- Small, sharp scissors

- ½ yard (45.5cm) grosgrain ribbon

- Fabric glue, such as Fabri-Tac or Gem-Tac

If you get the opportunity to flip through an issue of *Twist* magazine (or *Bop* or the ever popular *Tiger Beat*), I highly recommend it. My daughter Hannah reintroduced me to these glossy teeny-bopper tabloids a few years ago, and I'm not sure who likes them more: my tween or me!

These magazines are just plain fun. Devoid of the ugly gossip that appears in adult tabloids, the teen mags are filled with fun and funny stories, behind-the-scenes rumors, cute quizzes, and lots and lots of pictures of the latest teen heart-throbs. This headband was literally "torn" from the pages of one of Hannah's magazines. After selecting my "material" I laminated the pages with iron-on vinyl to make the paper durable. (Although the iron-on vinyl is normally used with fab-ric, I was happy to discover that it also works with paper.) This headband is so easy; you can make a special one for each new crush!

1. Make your pattern: Trace the outline of an undecorated headband
by drawing around the edges as
you "roll" the headband across
your paper. You will have drawn
what the headband would look
like if it were flattened out. Cut
out the shape, leaving plenty of
extra room around it.

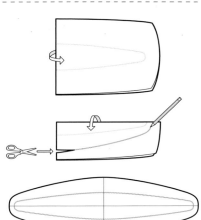

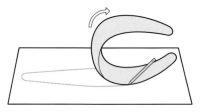

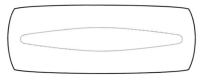

2. Fold the shape in half widthwise
(making sure to match up the
edges of the outline), then fold it
again lengthwise. Draw a line
about ¾" (2cm) from the thin end
of the headband outline, widen-
ing the margin so the line is about
1¼" (3cm) from the middle part
of the headband outline. (Since
the headband is thin at the ends
and wider at the middle, you
want to graduate the flap you're
drawing so there will be enough
material, but not too much, to
neatly cover the headband.) With
the paper still folded, trim the
pattern at this line.

3. "Laminate" magazine pages: You
will need 2 pages from the magazine to cover the headband.
Either use 2 pages that are printed
on one large sheet, like a center-
fold, or place 2 pages right next
to each other before you iron on
the vinyl. Apply the vinyl following the package instructions.

4. Use a couple pieces of cellophane tape to secure the pattern
to the laminated material, then
cut out the headband "fabric"
along the pattern edges.

5. Place a piece of double-sided tape
along the top of the headband in
the middle. Center the headband
on the magazine cutout. Cut slits
in the magazine cutout to the edge
of the headband every 1¼" (3cm)
or so, making small sections of the
flaps to fold over the back of the
headband. Small, sharp scissors
work well for this.

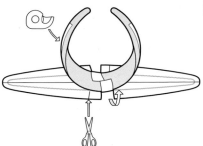

Continue clipping and folding until the flaps cover the back of the
headband all the way around.

6. Once all the little flap pieces are
folded over, use double-sided
tape to hold them down. Work
with small sections of material,
using small pieces of tape so you
can neatly and tightly cover the
headband.

7. Cover the inside seams with a
length of grosgrain ribbon. (Use a
little piece of double-sided tape
to "hem" the raw ends of the ribbon before you glue it down.)
Spread glue out across the back
of the ribbon so it is saturated,
then glue the ribbon in place.
Allow the glue to dry completely.

5

heart attack
gifts from the heart

Perhaps no gift is more significant than one given to say, "I love you." Of course, there is a holiday devoted to this, and all the gifts in this chapter make great Valentine's Day presents. But they're are also good anytime gifts. Many of them can be made in less than an hour, so spreading the love has never been easier.

The Heart-Felt Gloves on page 96, for example, show you how to turn an ordinary pair of gloves into something unique in just three steps. The Sweet-Heart Sachets on page 86, made from vintage dishtowels, remind me of Valentine's cookies and are just as yummy. And you'll want to make a bunch of the easy personalized Charming Necklaces on page 89. The charms are made out of Shrinky Dinks, so they take very little time but actually look quite sophisticated. After all, making something special doesn't have to be hard, and neither does saying "I love you."

Sweet-Heart Sachets

finished measurements

5" x 4½" (12.5cm x 10cm)

supplies (for 1 sachet)

- Two 6" x 12" (15cm x 30.5cm) dishtowel pieces
- Sewing machine
- Thread
- Iron and ironing board
- Small spoon or funnel
- 1 ounce (30g) loose dried lavender
- ½–1 cup (115–235mL) loose rice or flax seed (optional)

Made from new and vintage dishtowels, these small sachets are stuffed with lavender and look and smell great in a bedroom or bathroom. They also make sweet gifts. I used some dishtowel scraps left over from other projects to whip these up. I love the antique look, and the linen lets the fragrant dried flowers "breathe." You can also fill the hearts with dried chamomile or rose buds, or mix in some rice or flax seed if you want a lighter scent. Stack a few sachets together, then wrap them in a cellophane bag tied with a silk ribbon. A perfect little gift for the sweethearts in your life.

1. Out of scrap paper, make a heart pattern for your sachet. (The heart I used was approximately 5⅝" x 5⅝" [14.3cm x 14.3cm].)

2. Using your pattern, cut out 2 hearts from the dishtowel scraps, paying attention to any design or writing you want to feature.

3. With right sides facing each other, sew the 2 hearts together using a ¼" (6mm) seam allowance, leaving about 1¾" (4.5cm) open on one of the sides.

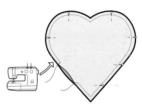

4. Trim the curved seam allowances to ⅛" (3mm). Trim the bottom corner point, and clip the inside point at the top of the heart to ease turning.

5. Turn the heart right side out, and fold in the extra seam allowance at the opening. Press.

6. Topstitch ¼" (6mm) from the edge to create a border around the heart, still leaving the side open. (If desired, you can add a second stitch border by stitching again very close the edge.)

7. Use a small spoon or funnel to add the lavender or any other fragrant dried flower. (If you are adding rice or flax seed, make the mixture first, before you fill the sachet.) Pin the opening closed, then stitch it closed, matching the seams and backstitching at the beginning and end.

not so humble beginnings

• • • • • • • •

The modern dishtowel, called a tea towel in England, dates back to the eighteenth century. In British homes, the mistress of the house used these fine handmade linen cloths to dry precious bone china and tea accessories, a delicate task they were leery to entrust to their servants.

Charming Necklace

Charming Necklace

finished measurements

Black and white fabric twine—25"
(63.5cm); pink fabric twine—16"
(40.5cm); charms—⅝" (1.5cm) in
diameter

supplies (for 1 necklace)

- Computer with inkjet printer
  (optional)

- Fine-line permanent marker

- Shrinkable plastic sheet, such as
  Shrinky Dinks Frosted Ruff N'
  Ready plastic sheets (Resources,
  page 118)

- 1½" (3.8cm) circle or heart paper
  punch, often used for
  scrapbooking (optional)

- 5mm hole punch, or standard ¼"
  (6mm) hole punch

- Oven

- Smooth-bottomed drinking
  glass or ceramic tile

- 5.5mm open jump ring

- Jewelry pliers

- Scraps of fabric for stringing
  charm, approximately 2" x 36"
  (5cm x 91cm)

- Iron and ironing board

- Rotary cutter and self-healing
  mat (optional)

- Waxed or parchment paper
  (optional)

- White glue, such as Elmer's Glue,
  and disposable plastic tub
  (optional)

- Small jewelry clasps (optional)

A store in my town sells beautiful charm necklaces made by jewelry designer Heather Moore. They're popular with moms I know, who often get their children's initials engraved on the charms and wear several at once. The charms for this project, strung on fabric instead of gold chains, were inspired by those necklaces, and they can be personalized with initials, names, or loving words. And the best part is . . . they're made from Shrinky Dinks, the "magical" shrinking plastic that made its debut in 1973!

Today, shrinkable plastic sheets can be used with top-loading inkjet printers and come in all sorts of colors and finishes, so feel free to experiment. I just used a sheet of the original "Frosted Ruff N' Ready" plastic, but for hand drawn designs, you can even make your own (Trash to Tiny Treasures, opposite). Happy shrinking!

1. Design your charm on the computer or by hand. Your design will shrink to about one-third of its original size, so make sure to account for this. Print out your design, or draw it using a permanent marker, on the rough side of the plastic sheet, and carefully cut out the charm. Scrapbooking paper punches work well to give you a "perfect" shape.

2. Using a hole punch, punch a hole near the top, at least ³⁄₁₆" (8mm) in from the edge of the charm. This must be done before you bake the charm.

3. Following the package instructions, bake and enjoy the show!

4. After removing your charm from the oven, place a heavy heat resistant object, such as a smooth-bottomed drinking glass or ceramic tile, on top of the charm to keep it nice and flat. When the charm is cool, add a jump ring using jewelry pliers.

5. Make a fabric necklace for the charm: With wrong sides together, fold a strip of fabric in half lengthwise and iron flat. To facilitate cutting, fold the fabric over again, widthwise. Measure ⅛" (3mm) over from the long folded edge, then cut a narrow folded strip using scissors or a rotary cutter and self-healing mat.

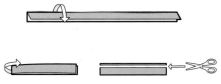

String the charm on the fabric as is, or use it to make a piece of twine, as described in the next step.

trash to tiny treasures

Make your own Shrinky Dinks from #6 plastic containers. (Look for the "6" inside the recycling symbol, stamped into the plastic.) Containers at salad bars are often made from this kind of plastic and will shrink up in the oven just like premade shrinkable plastic sheets. Use a 350-degree-Fahrenheit (175°C) oven and bake on a flat cookie sheet for a few minutes, until the plastic begins to curl, then flattens back out. Try this with hand-drawn designs; salad containers are not recommended for use with your printer!

great moments in
SHRINKY DINKS
HISTORY

1974: Using a toaster oven, Shrinky Dinks are demonstrated at Toy Fair in New York City.

1981: Colorforms, one of the first companies to license Shrinky Dinks, introduces Smurf Shrinky Dinks, its biggest seller.

2000: Shrinky Dinks go up in the Space Shuttle Atlantis as part of a first-grade science experiment. The children wanted to see if the plastic would shrink in space after being exposed to extreme temperatures . . . it didn't.

2002: The first Shrinky Dink Art Invitational is held, in which professional artists are required to create original works out of Shrinky Dinks plastic.

2007: Shrinky Dinks are used by medical engineers at the University of California, Merced, to make molds for microfluidics research.

2008: Sales of retail Shrinky Dinks products, since 1973, reach an estimated $150 million.

6. Make fabric twine (optional): Place a sheet of waxed or parchment paper on your work surface. Prepare a diluted glue mixture in the drinking glass or disposable plastic container, adding 1 part water to 3 parts glue. Dip your fingers in the mixture and roll the strip of fabric between your thumb and fingers. The fabric will fray a bit, but just keep adding the glue mixture until you get a nice, smooth piece of "twine." Let the twine dry, trim the ends, and then use it to string your charm.

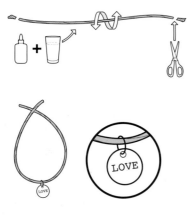

7. Put clasps on the necklace, following the package instructions, or leave the fabric as is to be tied around the neck.

honey, I shrunk . . . everything!

Shrinky Dinks were "invented" in 1973 by Betty Morris, a Cub Scout leader and stay-at-home mom. After seeing an article in a craft magazine involving tracing on plastic lids and shrinking them in the oven, Morris and her co-leader, Kathryn Bloomberg, introduced the project to their scouts. The boys were so excited by the activity, the women decided to create a product out of large sheets of the shrinkable plastic. They sold their first kits (packages of the plastic and project ideas that they had assembled themselves) at the Brookfield Square Mall in Wisconsin. Morris says she knew she was onto something when the Boy Scouts started fighting one another for the leftover scraps!

Wink, Wink Eye Mask

Wink, Wink Eye Mask

finished measurements

8" x 3¼" (20.5cm x 8.3cm)

supplies

- Eye Mask pattern template (page 125)

- ¼ yard (23cm) fabric for the front of the eye mask

- ¼ yard (23cm) lining fabric, such as a soft sheet

- ¼ yard (23cm) craft batting

- Cucumber slices

- Paper towel

- Scanner and printer

- 1 sheet T-shirt transfer paper for dark fabrics

- Iron and ironing board

- Sewing machine and matching thread

- 1 yard (91cm) elastic, approximately ½" (13mm) wide

Pamper someone you love with this one-of-a-kind refreshing eye mask. The cool cucumbers are actually iron-on transfers made from scans of real cucumber slices. Even though I wasn't working on a particularly dark fabric, I printed the cucumbers using T-shirt transfer paper made for dark material to make the cucumbers really pop.

Of course, an eye mask should not only be cute on the outside, but also very cozy and soft on the inside! For the lining, I used a super-soft, worn pink sheet that had outlived its usefulness on my daughter's bed. You can use any soft cotton or flannel, but recycling an old sheet will give the mask the comfy feel that can only be achieved by washing cotton bed linens hundreds of times! Just talking about those soft sheets makes me sleepy.

1. Photocopy the eye mask pattern template at the recommended percentage, and cut out the paper pattern. Use the pattern to cut out the following:

   Eye mask front

   Eye mask back, out of contrasting fabric

   Eye mask batting

2. Make cucumber transfers: Using paper towel, pat dry a few cucumber slices, then place them directly on your scanner. Scan and print a few samples on scrap paper. Once you are happy with the images, print them out on the T-shirt transfer. (If you do not have a scanner, a copy store can scan and print out the images for you, or use preprinted cucumber slice images.)

   Carefully cut out the cucumber slice images. Peel off the backing paper and center the cucumbers, right side up, on the right side of the eye mask front. (Use guides on template if needed, and remember that the finished eye mask will be ½" [13mm] smaller all the way around after it is sewn.) Iron on the cucumber images following the package instructions.

3. Pin the batting to the wrong side of the eye mask front. Baste in place using a ¼" (6mm) seam allowance, sewing on the front side of the mask.

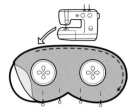

4. Attach elastic: Cut 2 lengths of elastic, each approximately 14" (35.5cm) long. (You may want to make the elastic a ½" [13mm] longer or shorter depending on how tight you want the mask to fit.) Using the markings on the template as your guide, pin the elastic to the *right side* of the eye mask front, lining up the raw edges. It will look like you are attaching the elastic across the *front* of the eye mask at this point, but when you finish, the elastic will be in the proper place on the back of the mask. Baste the elastic in place using a ¼" (6mm) seam allowance.

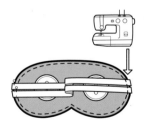

5. Attach the eye mask back: With right sides together, pin the eye mask back to the eye mask front. Beginning at the top right corner, stitch the eye mask together using a ½" (13mm) seam allowance, leaving about 4" (10cm) open at the top of the mask. Backstitch at the beginning and end of the seam. Clip into the seam allowance around the curve of the nose area to ease turning, and trim the seam allowances around the outside curves and sides to ¼" (6mm).

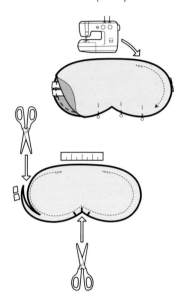

6. Turn the mask right side out, carefully pushing out the curves. Once you're happy with the shape, gently press the edges with your iron, being careful to avoid ironing directly on the cucumber transfers.

7. To finish the mask, fold in the ½" (13mm) seam allowance at the opening and pin closed. Topstitch the opening closed and continue around the entire mask, stitching close to the edge.

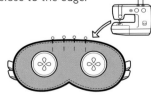

Heart-Felt Gloves

finished measurements
heart appliqué—⅞" x ¾" (2.2cm x 2cm)

supplies

- Scissors or heart-shaped scrapbooking punch
- Felt in a contrasting color
- 1 pair knit gloves
- Tennis ball
- Embroidery floss and needle

Is there anything more fun than making something super cute that also happens to be really, really easy? These gloves are exactly that kind of project, and they're sure to tickle your creative fancy. They are also the perfect little something to give when you want to send some extra Xs and Os without too much fuss.

Just start with a pair of plain gloves, then add some colorful hearts made out of felt. Stitch on the little adornments using a blanket stitch, and in thirty minutes or less, your gifts are ready to give. Whoever gets them will feel warm and cozy—and definitely loved!

1. Cut out 2 felt hearts, each approximately ⅞" x ¾" (2.2cm x 2cm). (I used a heart punch made for scrapbooking to cut out 2 identical hearts.)

2. Place the tennis ball inside one of the gloves, as if you were darning a pair of socks. The ball will help you sew the heart to the front of the glove only, without going through both the front and back layers of fabric. Place the heart in the desired location on the glove and stick a pin straight through the heart into the tennis ball to keep the heart in place.

3. Separate the embroidery floss into a 3-ply strand and thread an embroidery needle. Then sew the heart to the glove using a blanket stitch. Refer to Blanket Stitch How-To, for more information on this type of stitch. Knot the thread ends, and trim the thread.

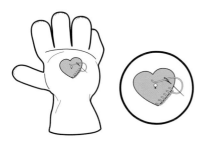

4. Repeat steps 2 and 3 on the remaining glove.

Blanket Stitch How-To

The blanket stitch is an embroidery stitch often used to finish the thick edges of an unhemmed blanket. It is also used for appliqué or just for decoration. For this project, start your blanket stitch with your thread coming up through the glove fabric right at the edge of the felt heart. Poke your needle and thread back through the heart, about ⅛" (3mm) above the edge and a tiny bit over to the right. Bring your needle straight down, but as the needle is pulled through, keep the thread under the needle point. Pull the stitch to form a loop. Repeat, stitching all the way around the heart.

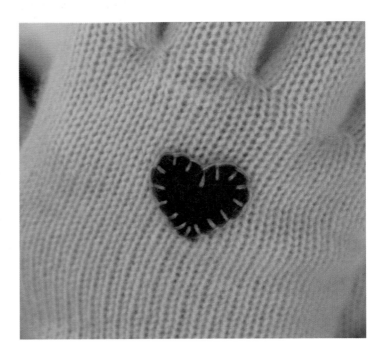

Hot Lips Pillow

finished measurements
25" x 12" (63.5cm x 30.5cm)

supplies

- Hot Lips pattern template (page 126)

- ½ yard (45.5cm) stretch vinyl (if using a fabric with a pattern or repeating design, you may need more yardage)

- Scotch matte-finish "Magic" tape

- Sewing machine

- Thread

- Parchment paper

- Pen

- 1-pound (454g) bag polyester craft stuffing

I grew up in Colorado in a pretty ordinary 1960s ranch house. But my parents had surprisingly modern sensibilities when it came to design, especially for a couple of suburbanites who had never left Denver. Their house was featured in a local magazine when I was young, and I can still remember the photo of their sleek living room, complete with a low-slung olive-green couch, gourd-shaped lamp, and shag carpeting. In the '70s, my parents updated the house again, adding all sorts of mod accessories, including an oversized throw pillow shaped like a pair of lips. It was made from some sort of stretch felt material, and it always put a smile on my face.

These Hot Lips are my version of that groovy throw pillow. Mine are made from shiny red stretch vinyl, but they could also be made out of felt or T-shirt jersey material—any fabric with a little give. Mom and Dad, this pillow is for you, sealed with a kiss.

1. Photocopy the Hot Lips pattern template at the recommended percentage, and cut out the paper pattern. Fold the fabric in half, right sides together, and tape the Hot Lips pattern to the fabric. (The tape allows you to avoid using pins, which can leave holes in the vinyl fabric.) Cut out 2 lip-shaped pieces.

2. With right sides still facing, stitch the 2 lip pieces together using a ½" (13mm) seam allowance, leaving a 4" (10cm) opening on both the top and bottom section of the lips, as shown. The openings should begin a little in from one corner to ensure the corners themselves are stitched by machine. (If necessary, hold the 2 pieces together with a few pieces of tape, instead of pins, before you sew.)

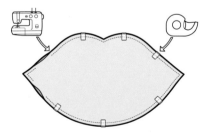

3. Clip around the top of the lips, at the corners, and the curves to ease turning. Trim the seam allowances to ¼" (6mm), but *do not trim the seams near the openings*.

4. Turn the pillow right side out, finger pressing the edges so the lips are shaped nicely and evenly. Using the Hot Lips pattern template as a guide, cut out a piece of parchment paper that is the same size as the *finished* pillow, and draw the center lip line onto the paper. Use a pen or thin permanent marker to draw all lines, as a pencil can rub off and leave marks on the fabric and thread. Tape the parchment paper directly on top of the pillow, lining up all edges.

5. Sew the center lip line on the pillow by stitching directly on top of the parchment paper, following the drawn line. The parchment paper guide will help you sew on the slippery vinyl fabric and will also let you sew a "perfect" center lip line. After sewing, carefully rip the parchment paper away from the fabric, leaving only the stitching.

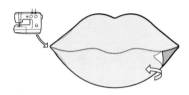

6. Tightly stuff both sections of the lips, working so that the stuffing is as smooth and free of lumps as possible. Once the pillow looks the way you want, slip stitch the open edges closed on each section. Knot the ends, and trim all threads.

6

holiday hoopla
gifts of the season

Too often the holidays are more mayhem than merry. So add some of the joy back into your holiday season by getting your creative juices flowing! You might think you don't have time to make your own presents for the holidays, but actually, many of the gifts featured here will take less time (and will certainly be more fun) than facing the throngs at the mall.

The Fabric Note Cards on page 102, for example, are my surefire holiday gift. I usually make a big batch then dole them out to teachers, neighbors, and holiday hostesses. The Slick Stocking on page 114 is a new twist on an old tradition (it's made from shiny oilcloth) and can be personalized to be even more special and unique.

The one project that will require some time (and plenty of dishtowels) is the quilt on page 109, but trust me, it's worth it. The quilt can be made from new or vintage dishtowels, or a combination of both. As quilts go, it's a pretty simple one. It's also the perfect size to snuggle under. And isn't feeling the warmth of loved ones what the season is really all about? Making *something*, whether it's a holiday card, a bunch of cookies, or a handmade gift will bring you and others joy—and that's truly, simply sublime.

Fabric Note Cards

These note cards are such a fun way to use up scraps of fabric, and they're especially appealing when grouped together. In fact, half the fun of making these cards is mixing and matching all your fabrics until you come up with a "color story" that pleases you. The cards make great "anyone" gifts, so you'll want to make plenty around the holidays. And don't be surprised if they disappear quicker than freshly baked Christmas cookies—no matter how many you make, you'll wish you had more to give away.

finished measurements

5½" x 4½" (14cm x 11.5cm)

supplies

- Scraps of cotton fabric, at least 1" (2.5cm) wider and taller than the front of the card

- Iron and ironing board

- Scissors (or a rotary cutter, straightedge, and self-healing mat)

- Blank white fold-over note cards (available at office supply stores such as Staples or craft stores such as Michael's)

- Cardboard box, such as a large shoebox (optional)

- Repositionable spray adhesive, such as Spray Mount glue

1. Iron the fabric to get out all the wrinkles, then, keeping in mind the design you want to feature, cut a swatch of fabric that is bigger than the front of the card.

2. Isolate the design, then trim the fabric on at least 2 adjoining sides to "frame" the image. You can then use the cut edges as a guide when you glue the fabric on the card.

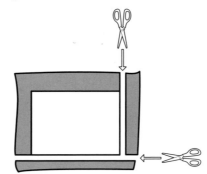

3. Place the fabric swatch, right side down, in a large open box or on several sheets of plain paper, and spray the back of it with spray adhesive. Place a blank folded card face down on the fabric, lining up the cut sides

with the sides of the card, and press and smooth the card with your hands. Allow the glue to dry a little, then cleanly trim the extra material around the edges of the card. (A rotary cutter and straightedge work well for this, but you can also just use a pair of scissors.)

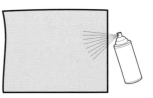

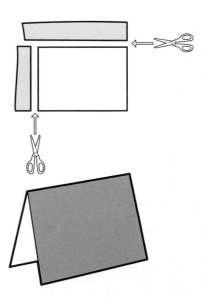

Stuffed Ornaments

finished measurements

girl ornament—2 ⅜" x 6 ½" (6cm x 16.5cm); dog ornament—2 ¼" x 4" (5.5cm x 10cm)

supplies (for 1 ornament)

- Photo

- Computer with scanner and printer

- 2 printable fabric sheets (often used for quilting)

- 8 ½" x 11" (21.5cm x 28cm) piece of fabric for backing

- Approximately ¼ yard (23cm) craft batting (¼" [6mm] loft)

- Sewing machine

- Thread

- Small, sharp scissors

- 12" (30.5cm) embroidery floss or thin ribbon

Turn your favorite family photos into one-of-a-kind 3-D ornaments. These little "pillow people" are made with fabric transfer paper and stuffed with quilt batting. They make great holiday gifts, especially for grandparents, and kids love them, too! Use a piece of embroidery thread or a thin ribbon to make a loop so your ornament can hang on a hook or tree. Make one for each family member—and don't forget Fido!

1. Scan the picture you want to use into your computer, and size it to your liking. (Full body images work well. The ornaments pictured here measure 4" [10cm] and 6½" [16.5cm] tall.) Print out the image on scrap paper first to check the size, then print it out on the fabric sheet. (If you're making more than one ornament, you can lay out 2 images on one page.)

2. Trim the photo image, leaving a good 1" (2.5cm) border or more all around. Cut out a piece of backing fabric the same size. Then assemble the ornament for sewing by layering a piece of batting between the front and back pieces. You will be making a little "sandwich," with the right sides of both the front and back pieces facing out, and the batting in between. Use a few pins to hold all the layers together, pinning in the extra border area, not through the main body.

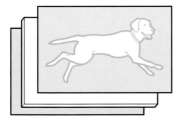

3. Starting almost at the very top, use your sewing machine to carefully stitch around the image outline. Stitch almost completely around, leaving a small ½" (13mm) section open at the top of the ornament. Trim all threads. Carefully trim all the way around the ornament (even at the unsewn top). Cut very close to the stitching to make a sharp, clean, silhouette.

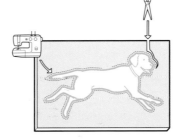

4. Make a loop out of embroidery thread or ribbon, and using the point of your scissors or a sharp wooden skewer, tuck the raw ends inside the opening at the top of the ornament. Sew the top of the ornament closed. Stitch forward and back a few times to secure the loop. Trim all threads.

✷ FRAY-FREE EDGES

Store-bought printable fabric sheets are often treated with a finish that coincidentally prevents the edges from fraying. So if you want to make sure that your edges are "fray free," make the back (as well as the front) of your ornament using a printable fabric sheet. Just scan or copy a swatch of material, and then print it out on the fabric sheet. The resulting "fabric" will look identical to the real thing but won't fray.

Fabric Nesting Bowls

finished measurements

small bowl—4" x 2³⁄₁₆" (10cm x 5.6cm); large bowl—6" x 3³⁄₁₆" (15cm x 8cm)

supplies (for 1 bowl)

- Plastic bowl for mold (preferably a square bowl with 4 sides)
- Paper to make pattern, such as graph paper
- Ruler and pencil
- Approximately ¼ yard (23cm) each of cotton fabrics in 2 different patterns
- Iron and ironing board
- Parchment or waxed paper
- Large bottle of white glue, approximately 16 ounces (473mL), such as Elmer's Glue
- Disposable plastic container with lid for glue mixture
- Plastic spoon
- 1 or 2 craft sponge brushes
- Tall plastic cup
- Sharp, straight-edged kitchen knife
- Long wooden skewer
- Small, sharp scissors

Like many of my fellow crafters and sewers, I'm a fabric junkie. If it weren't for the fact that my family deserves at least a few corners that are "fabric free," I'd be quite content to fill every extra cupboard in the house with piles of fabric. So I try to control myself when I see material I love. I'll buy a fat quarter, or sometimes just a ½ yard (45.5cm), hoping it won't take up too much room.

Sometimes I take out all my fabric and play with the swatches like they're doll clothes or paint chips. Okay, I know that's a little embarrassing, but it was during one of these fabric fiestas that I came up with the idea for fabric nesting bowls. These bowls are made with contrasting scraps of fabric and ordinary craft glue—like papier-mâché, but with cloth—and are the perfect way to use small bits of beautiful fabric.

1. Make a paper pattern for your bowl: For the side pattern, use a pencil to trace the edge of the bowl onto graph paper, then add ¼" (6mm) on each side and ½" (13mm) on the bottom. The top of the side pattern should be flush with the top of the bowl. For the bottom, trace around the bottom of the bowl at a sharp angle so the paper pattern will fit perfectly inside the bowl. Measure with a ruler and trim with scissors to fit if necessary.

2. Iron both pieces of fabric to get out all the wrinkles.

3. Cut out the fabric: Using the paper patterns, cut out 4 sides from one piece of fabric for the inside of the bowl. Cut out 4 sides and 2 square bottoms from the remaining fabric.

4. Make the glue mixture: Cover your workspace with a large piece of parchment or waxed paper. In a disposable container, mix 2 parts of glue with 1 part water. (You may need to add a little more water if the mixture is hard to spread.)

   Note: The glue mixture may seep through paper, so it's best to work on a washable surface such as formica.

5. Turn the bowl over, then begin gluing the pieces of fabric to the mold. Start by gluing the inside square bottom fabric face down onto the *out-side* bottom of the mold. (This way, when you remove the mold, the first layer of fabric will be right side up inside the bowl.) Use a sponge brush

to carefully cover the fabric with the glue mixture.

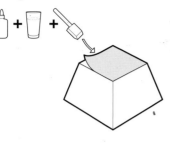

6. Add the inside side pieces of fabric: Brush the right side of the fabric with the glue mixture, then place it on the mold, right side down, aligning the raw top edge flush with the rim of the bowl. Neatly fold the edges of the bottom and the sides over the mold. Continue applying the inside side fabric pieces in this manner, neatly folding the sides and corners over each other. At the rim there will be little extra triangles of fabric where the sides meet. Don't worry about this; they will be trimmed later. Once all side pieces are in place, brush them again with another coat of the glue mixture.

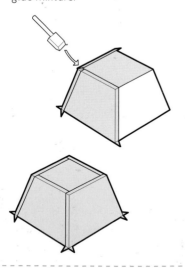

7. Repeat step 6 again, beginning with the outside side pieces. This time, however, make sure the side fabric pieces are right side out. (These pieces will form the outside of the bowl.)

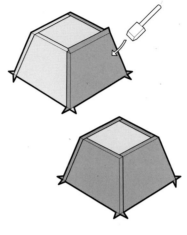

Once you have attached the outside side pieces, add the bottom square, right side up. This will cover all the layers to form a neat bottom.

8. Let the glue dry: Place a tall plastic cup under the mold to lift it off the table and facilitate drying. Depending on the size of your bowl and the weather, it will take several hours for your bowl to dry completely, but you want to remove it from the mold before it is totally dry. Check your bowl after 2–3 hours. When the fabric begins to stiffen and is no longer moist, but not bone dry, use a straight-edged knife or long wooden skewer to loosen the fabric from the plastic mold. Then use the knife or skewer to "pop" the fabric bowl off of the plastic mold. Allow the bowl to finishing drying completely.

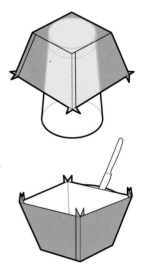

9. When the bowl is completely dry, trim the edges and corners with small, sharp scissors.

✳ IT'S HIP TO BE SQUARE

I used square-shaped four-sided plastic bowls for my molds, which are easier to find than you might think. I got mine at Pier 1, but I've seen them at Target, online, and even at my local grocery store.

Dishtowel Quilt

Dishtowel Quilt

finished measurements

60" x 60" (152.5cm x 152.5cm)

supplies

- Enough dishtowels to make twenty-five 13" x 13" (33cm x 33cm) squares (sometimes you can cut 2 squares from one dishtowel)

- 1 twin-size flat sheet (66" x 96" [167cm x 244cm]), for backing

- Iron and ironing board

- Rotary cutter, acrylic ruler (or square quilter's ruler), and self-healing mat

- Sewing machine

- Thread

- Low-loft (approximately ¼" [6mm]) quilt batting for twin-size bed (72" x 90" [183cm x 229cm])

- Masking tape

- Quilter's safety pins

- 3 skeins embroidery thread in a complementary color

- Large embroidery needle or curved quilt needle

- Walking foot attachment for your sewing machine (optional)

I had never made a quilt before—I've always been too scared! But with the help of my friend Tammy, who is an amazing seamstress, I finally did it. This quilt is a traditional patchwork pattern, five squares wide and fives squares tall, and is hand tied (a quilting shortcut; page 113). It's the perfect size for a throw or picnic blanket, or to fold up at the end of a twin bed. It's made from new and old dishtowels, many of which I collected over the years.

I learned a lot of things from making this quilt. First, don't be shy when it comes to asking for help. My friend's assistance and advice were invaluable—as were the several calls I made to my local quilt shop. Second, don't be afraid to try new things or cut up treasured fabrics. The finished quilt was proof to me that sometimes it pays to go beyond your comfort zone. And finally, take a minute to stand back and enjoy the fruits of your labor, whether admiring the quilt you finally tackled, savoring the pie you baked, or delighting in the relationships you've built with family and friends. No matter the season, get wrapped up in something that tickles your fancy. It will keep you warm year-round.

1. Prepare the fabric: Wash, dry, and press the dishtowels and twin sheet.

2. Cut out twenty-five 13" x 13" (33cm x 33cm) squares from the dishtowels using a rotary cutter, acrylic ruler or square quilter's ruler, and cutting mat.

3. This is the fun part! Lay out your squares to create a design that is 5 squares wide by 5 squares tall. If you want to play around with the design, now is the time to do it!

4. Once you've finalized your design, attach scraps of paper or stickers to each square to label them as shown below, with rows from the top to bottom numbered 1–5, and the columns going across labeled a–e. You might be tempted to skip this step, but don't! It is important to label your squares before you stack them up so they don't get out of order.

1a	1b	1c	1d	1e
2a	2b	2c	2d	2e
3a	3b	3c	3d	3e
4a	4b	4c	4d	4e
5a	5b	5c	5d	5e

5. Remove the blocks from your work surface in rows, stacking 1a on top of 1b, 1b on top of 1c, and so on. Keep each row stack separate.

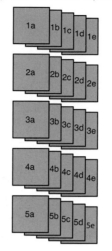

6. Now it's time to sew! With right sides together, stitch the first 2 blocks in the first row together, sewing the right-hand side of 1a to the left-hand side of 1b using a ½" (13mm) seam allowance. Continue sewing all the blocks in row 1 together to form a long 5-block strip. Sew each additional row together in the same manner to make a total of 5 separate strips. Press the seams in rows 1, 3, and 5 to the left. Press seams in rows 2 and 4 to the right. This will make the underside of the quilt less bulky.

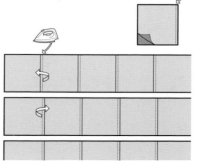

7. Sew the rows together. Start by sewing the bottom of row 1 to the top of row 2 with right sides together and a ½" (13mm) seam allowance, then the bottom of row 2 to the top of row 3, and so on. Press the seams to one side. Celebrate! You've made your quilt top! You've come this far, now keep going.

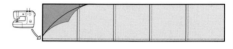

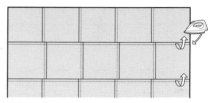

8. Prepare the backing and the batting: Cut the backing and batting each into a large 65" x 65" (165cm x 165cm) square.

9. Make the quilt sandwich: Put all 3 layers of your quilt together: the backing, the batting, and the quilt top. Start by smoothing out the backing, wrong side up, laying it out on a clean floor. Tape the backing fabric to the floor with strips of masking tape to hold it in place, taping the 2 side edges first, then the top and bottom. Make sure not to stretch the backing out of shape; keep it taut and square. Center the batting on

top of the backing material, then center the quilt top on top of the batting.

10. Baste all 3 layers together using quilter's safety pins. Start at the center of the quilt top and work your way to the edges, smoothing the fabric as you go. Place the pins about 5" (12.5cm) apart, all over the quilt.

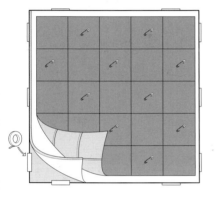

11. Once all the layers are basted together, remove the tape from the backing fabric—it's time to quilt! You will be hand-tying your quilt at each corner where 4 squares intersect. Thread two 6-strand pieces of embroidery floss on an embroidery needle or curved quilter's needle, but do not knot the ends. Starting at the intersection of squares in the middle of the quilt, insert your needle in the quilt top, pulling it through to the backing (going through all 3 layers), and leaving a 2" (5cm) tail.

Then poke your needle back up about ¼" (6mm) over from where you started. Cut the ends to measure 2" (5cm). You will now have 4 threads. Tie the ends together in a square knot (Quilting Shortcuts, opposite). Continue tying your quilt at each 4-corner intersection, working from the center out, and gently smoothing the fabric as you go. When you're all done, trim the ties to a uniform length, approximately 1" (2.5cm) long.

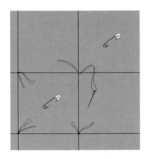

12. Prepare your quilt for binding: After you've hand-tied your quilt, you'll notice that the backing and batting will have shrunk up a bit. First, trim your batting to be flush with the quilt top. To do this, slide the cutting mat between the batting and the backing and use a rotary cutter and ruler to carefully trim the batting so it meets the quilt top edge. Do this all the way around the quilt. Now cut the backing to be 2" (5cm) outside the edge of the

quilt top, again using a rotary cutter, ruler, and mat.

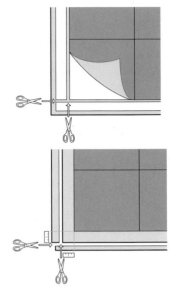

13. Make the binding: Starting on a side edge, fold the excess backing fabric in half, toward the quilt, and finger press in place. (You can also use a few pins to temporarily hold it down.) Now fold the backing fabric on the perpendicular edge over in the same manner. Fold this side over again to create a double-folded 1" (2.5cm) binding. Fold the corner point up as shown, at a 45-degree angle, then fold the first single-folded side edge over again, another 1" (2.5cm). You will now have made a mitered corner. Pin the folded sides and corner in place, and repeat folding over the binding and making the corners around the entire quilt. Press.

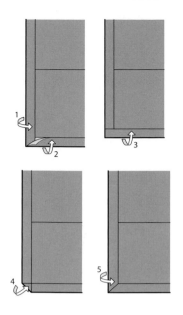

14. Last step! Sew the binding down by stitching very close to the binding edge. (You may want to use a walking-foot attachment to help feed the thick layers of fabric.) Begin sewing along a mitered corner first, then continue along one side of the quilt, backstitching at the beginning and end. Then start sewing again at the next corner, continuing on to the next side of the quilt. Continue all the way around the binding until all the corners and sides are sewn down.

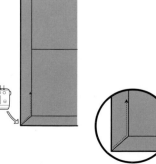

quilting shortcuts
. . . .

Quiltmaking requires a greater time investment than some other crafts, so this project uses several shortcuts to speed up the process.

Use one large piece of fabric for both the backing and binding. I used a twin sheet, which unlike ordinary fabric, is big enough to back the entire quilt without sewing several pieces together. Also, by cutting the fabric even larger than the quilt top, the extra material can be folded over the sides to bind all the layers and finish the edges.

Use safety pins to baste your quilt pieces together. For a quilt this size, and one that is not going to be quilted with intricate stitches, safety pins work fine, and they are quicker and easier than hand-basting.

Use a traditional hand-tying technique. I hand-tied this quilt using square knots to keep the quilt top, batting, and backing securely in place.

To tie a square knot, simply cross one thread over the other—right over left—to tie the first "half knot." Then, cross the threads left over right to make the second "half-knot." Pull the ends tight.

Yay! You did it— you made a quilt!

Slick Stocking

finished measurements
9¾" x 15¾" (24.5cm x 40cm)

supplies (for 1 stocking)
- Slick Stocking pattern templates (page 127)
- ½ yard (45.5cm) oilcloth for main stocking
- ¼ yard (23cm) oilcloth for contrasting cuff
- Scotch matte-finish "Magic" tape
- Sewing machine
- Thread
- Computer with inkjet printer
- 1 printable fabric sheet (often used for quilting)
- 8" (20.5cm) of ⅝"- (15mm-) wide grosgrain ribbon
- Pinking shears (optional)

I think Christmas stockings are about the sweetest things going. Although they are usually made from felt or wool, I wanted to try something different. My first idea was to make the stocking material out of sewn-together ribbons, but it just wasn't working. So I headed back to the drawing board (and back to my fabric closet!). Though I would normally never think of using oilcloth for this project, when forced to find an alternative to the ribbons, the cute cherry fabric practically leapt out and said, "Choose me!"

Sometimes creative roadblocks force you to back up, turn around, and head in a new direction. If you're lucky, you might even end up at a better destination.

1. Photocopy the Slick Stocking pattern templates, and cut out the paper patterns. Use the patterns to cut out 2 main stocking pieces and 2 contrasting cuffs from the oilcloth. Cut one set of pieces with the paper patterns reversed so that the pieces mirror each other and can be sewn together properly.

2. Tape the cuff to the stocking with the wrong side of the stocking facing the right side of the cuff, lining up the top raw edges, as shown. (The tape allows you to avoid using pins, which can leave holes in oilcloth.) Sew the cuff to the stocking using a ½" (13mm) seam allowance. Repeat with the remaining stocking and cuff pieces.

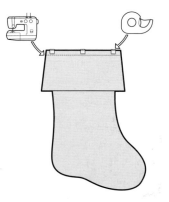

3. Turn both sewn pieces over so that the main stocking material is right side up. Flip the cuffs above the stockings, and finger press the seams up, toward the cuffs. The cuffs will look like they've been sewn on backward.

4. Tape the stocking pieces together, with right sides facing. Sew only the main stocking pieces together (do not sew the cuffs) using a ½" (13mm) seam allowance, starting and stopping at the seam where the cuffs have been sewn on, and backstitching at the beginning and end. Clip the stocking very close to the cuff edge, clipping almost all the way to the side seam, as shown.

wrapper's delight

· · · · · · · · · · · ·

Commercial wrapping paper, as we now know it, can be traced back to 1917 and a Kansas City store operated by Joyce C. Hall, the founder of Hallmark Cards. When the shop ran out of the red, white, and green tissue traditionally used during the holidays, Hall's brother scrambled and put out some envelope lining papers from France, selling the sheets for 10 cents a piece. The papers flew off the shelves, and a whole new industry was born.

6. Turn the stocking right side out. The cuff will now be wrong side up. "Hem" one side of the cuff by folding ¾" (2cm) of the cuff toward the wrong side of the fabric. Finger press the fold, then use a few pieces of tape to hold the "hem" in place. Repeat on the other side of the cuff.

on a printable fabric sheet using an inkjet printer. Cut out the tag and fold it in half. Remove the backing paper. Refer to Making Personalized Tags, page 64, for more information on tags.

8. With the stocking right side out and the toe pointing to the left, fold the top cuff down so it is right side up as well. Place the tag face down on the right-hand side of the cuff, in the middle, lining up raw edges. Pin the tag in place close to the edge.

5. Clip the curves and trim the seam allowance to ⅜" (9mm) at the toe and heel curves to facilitate turning.

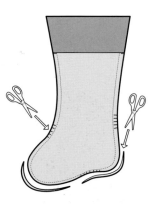

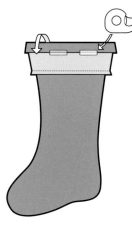

9. Fold the cuff back up so the wrong side of the cuff faces out. Stitch together the side cuff seams using a ½" (13mm) seam allowance, backstitching at the beginning and end and sewing all

7. Make the tag: Use your computer to design your tag. Print the tag

the way to the seam that connects the cuff to the stocking, but *not* over it, as shown. Trim threads and cut the cuff corners near the "hem" on a diagonal.

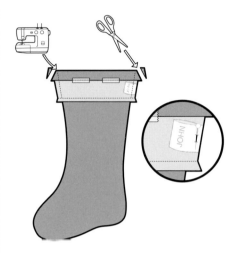

10. Remove the tape from the back of the cuff. Fold the cuff over the top of the stocking, so it is right side out, and then clip the inside side seams on a diagonal so they don't show at the top of the stocking.

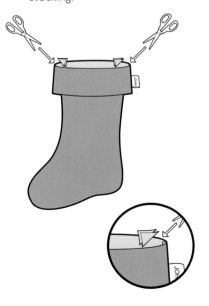

11. Make the loop: Fold the ribbon in half to make a loop at your desired length, and sew the bottom raw edges together using a ½" (13mm) seam allowance. Trim the raw edges with pinking shears or finish them with a zigzag stitch.

12. Place the loop inside the stocking and sew it in place on the "back" cuff, stitching back and forth to secure.

resources

WHERE TO GO WHEN YOU'RE LOOKING FOR:

fabrics

B&J FABRICS

www.bandjfabrics.com

Always at the top of my list when shopping for fabrics, this family-run store has been a mainstay in New York City's garment district for more than sixty years. They carry just about every type of fabric imaginable, including the stretch vinyl used for the Hot Lips pillow project and the Liberty of London cottons used to wrap the Fabric-Covered Soaps.

REPRODEPOT FABRICS

www.reprodepot.com

An online fabric store with a terrific collection of vintage reproduction and retro-themed textiles. They also stock buttons, ribbons, and other must-have sewing notions such as bias-tape-making tools and Jiffy Grip fabric. The website is fun and inspiring, and the staff is wonderful, too!

DENVER FABRICS

www.denverfabrics.com

Shop this online fabric store for a great selection of fabrics and supplies at discount prices. A good source for oilcloth.

PURL PATCHWORK

www.purlsoho.com

Sisters Joelle and Jennifer Hoverson opened this cozy fabric store in 2006 as the counterpart to their yarn shop, Purl, in downtown Manhattan. The shop specializes in materials made from natural fibers, and the website is a treasure trove of beautiful fabric designs. Don't miss their selection of Japanese imports.

OILCLOTH INTERNATIONAL

www.oilcloth.com

One of the largest wholesale distributors and manufacturers of oilcloth in the U.S. The company does not sell retail, but they are happy to help you find a store in your area that stocks their beautiful patterns.

notions and trimmings

THE SNAP SOURCE

www.snapsource.com

These snaps are the coolest! You'll use these long-prong fasteners in a million different ways. They are incredibly easy to put in and come in a huge variety of styles, colors, and sizes. The owner, Jeanine Twig, couldn't be nicer or more helpful. You can buy the snaps in fabric stores or place an order online.

M&J TRIMMING

www.mjtrim.com

Ribbons, buttons, belt buckles, and more. This trim store has it all, displayed on shelves that reach to the ceiling. If you can't make it to New York City, you can find almost everything you need on their website.

STEINLAUF AND STOLLER

www.steinlaufandstoller.com

I love this shop! This New York fabric district old-timer stocks everything from zippers to corset stays. Browsing through their online catalog is like entering a time warp. If you're looking for horsehair, they've got it! (Along with thousands of other items stocked for immediate delivery.)

other supplies and information

JUNE TAILOR

www.junetailor.com

You'll have loads of fun exploring all the unique products available from this well-known creative goods company that's been around for almost fifty years. June Tailor makes all sorts of quilting and craft supplies, including my favorite line of iron-on transfer papers and printable fabric sheets. The products are available on the web as well as in retail stores.

THERM O WEB

www.thermoweb.com

Visit Therm O Web's site to shop for all sorts of cool craft products, including the iron-on vinyl used for the His (and Hers) Washroom Bag, Heartthrob Headband, and Wonder Wallet.

SHRINKY DINKS

www.shrinkydinks.com

This is your link to the magical world of Shrinky Dinks, the original shrinkable plastic company. The range of products available will blow your mind! From colored plastics to jewelry supplies to use with your designs—you'll find everything you need to have a shrinking good time.

MOVERS SUPPLY HOUSE

www.moversupply.com

This down-and-dirty moving supply company is located in the Bronx, just twenty minutes outside of New York City. But you don't have to visit in person to purchase quilted moving blankets (they refer to them as furniture pads) and other moving supplies. Their online catalog is amazing— you'll come across stuff you never knew existed, like 1"- (2.5cm-) wide rubber bands that are over a yard (91cm) long!

FINDTAPE.COM

www.findtape.com

If you like sticky stuff, this is the place for you. This site sells over 350 different kinds of tape in thousands of colors and sizes. Tape junkies, rejoice!

WILTON FOOD CRAFTS

www.wilton.com

This premiere baking supply company carries silicone baking cups like those used for the Hello, Cupcake! Pincushion. It also stocks just about every other baking product imaginable. Careful—this site is as addictive as sugar!

TRIMWEAVER

www.trimweaver.com

This is one of my new favorite craft supply sites. Known for their hair products, they have a great assortment of headbands, barrettes, and clips just waiting to be decorated! (They carry the 2"- [5cm-] wide plastic bands used for the Heartthrob Headband project.) The site also features much more, including fabric and jewelry findings at prices that can't be beat.

JO-ANN FABRIC AND CRAFT STORES

www.joann.com

Another great source for craft and sewing supplies, such as quilt batting, fiberfill stuffing, and just about anything else you'll need to turn your craft corner into a fully stocked DIY oasis. You may find their website even more manageable than their giant stores.

CREATE FOR LESS

www.createforless.com

More than fifty thousand craft supplies at discount prices. They've got everything you're looking for, from paper punches to fabric glue and spray adhesive.

FISKARS

www.fiskars.com

Using the right cutting tools will make you feel like the queen of crafts. So go ahead, indulge in a pair of smooth-as-silk Teflon scissors, or treat yourself to a pinking blade for your rotary cutter. The site features descriptions of all the different Fiskars products with links to local retailers. Who knew there were so many ways to cut things?

templates

The following templates will need to be photocopied and enlarged to the appropriate size before you pin them to your fabric. In small quantities, for personal use, you are free to make photocopies from this book.

hello cupcake! pincushion
photocopy at 200% magnification

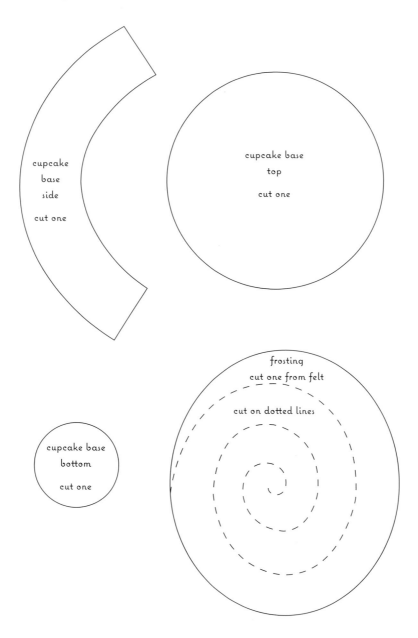

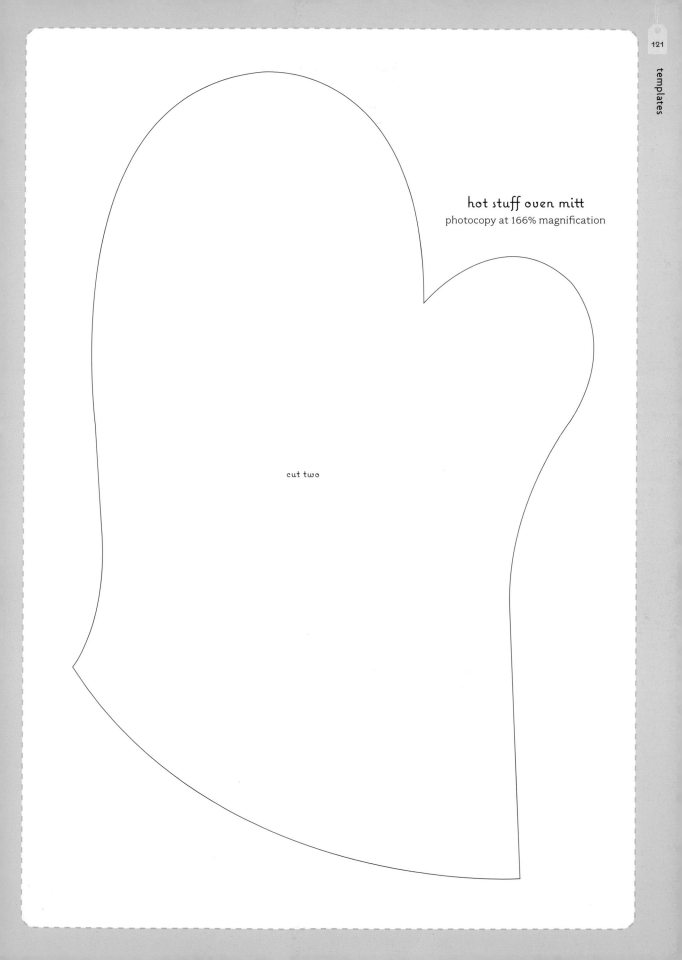

hot stuff oven mitt
photocopy at 166% magnification

cut two

dishtowel slippers

photocopy at 250% magnification

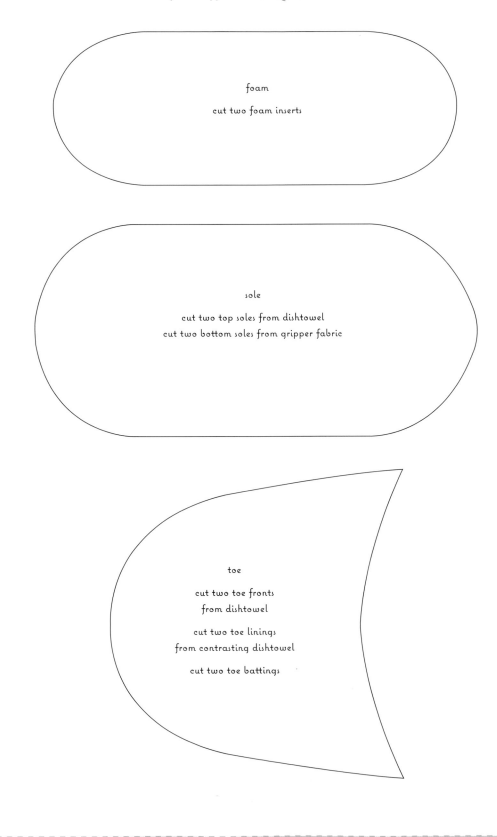

foam

cut two foam inserts

sole

cut two top soles from dishtowel
cut two bottom soles from gripper fabric

toe

cut two toe fronts
from dishtowel

cut two toe linings
from contrasting dishtowel

cut two toe battings

life's a ball! photo baseball
photocopy at 100% magnification

cut one
baseball piece out of
photo fabric

cut one
baseball piece out of
contrasting fabric

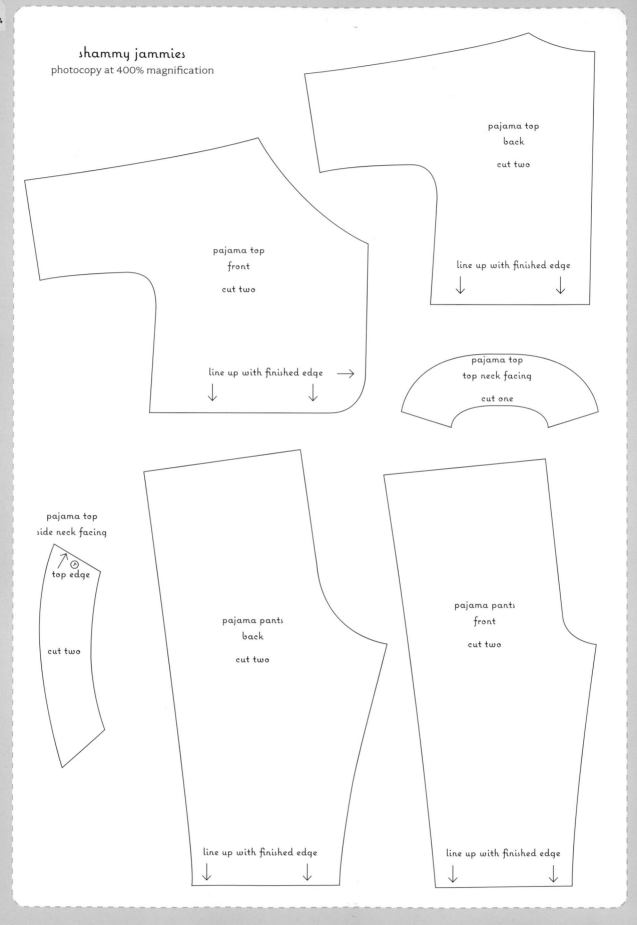

shammy jammies
photocopy at 400% magnification

pajama top
back

cut two

line up with finished edge

pajama top
front

cut two

line up with finished edge →

pajama top
top neck facing

cut one

pajama top
side neck facing

top edge

cut two

pajama pants
back

cut two

pajama pants
front

cut two

line up with finished edge

line up with finished edge

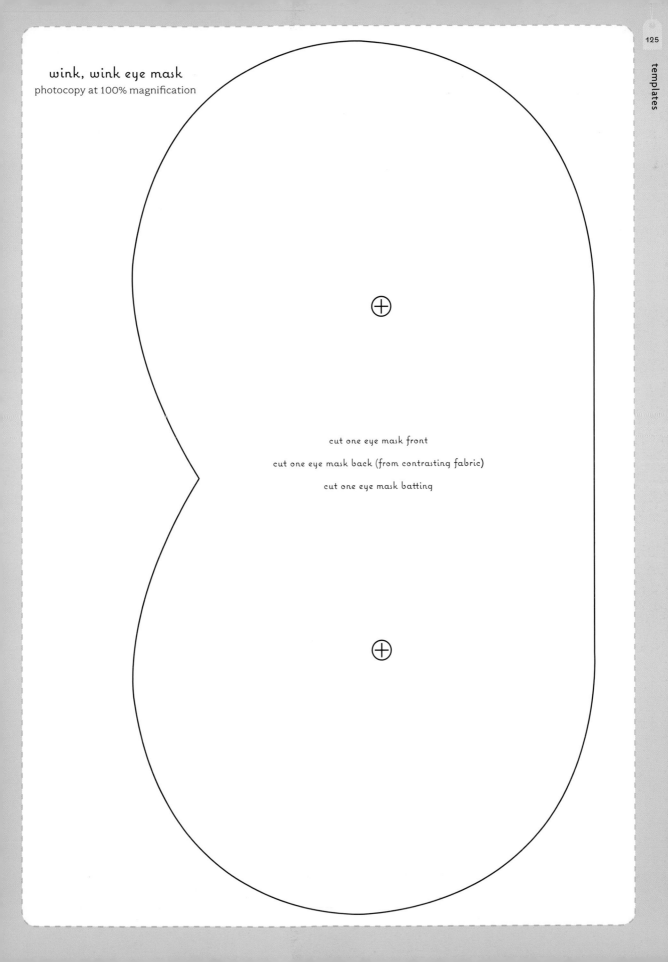

wink, wink eye mask
photocopy at 100% magnification

cut one eye mask front

cut one eye mask back (from contrasting fabric)

cut one eye mask batting

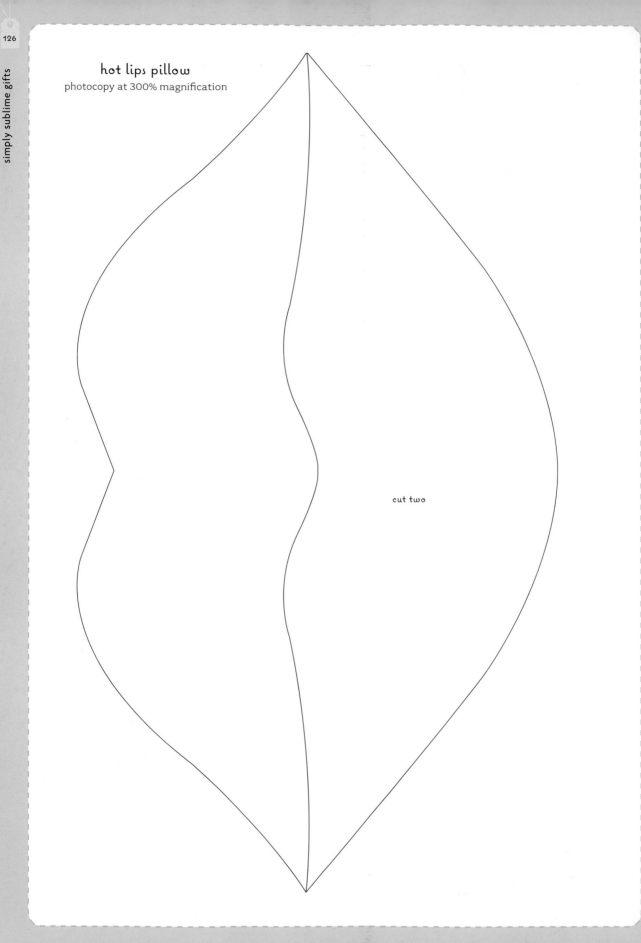

hot lips pillow
photocopy at 300% magnification

cut two

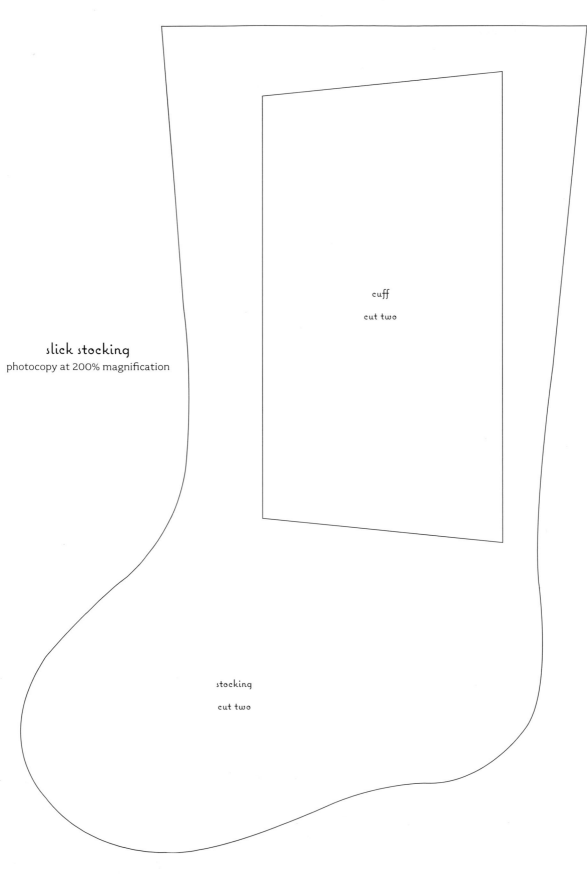

cuff

cut two

slick stocking
photocopy at 200% magnification

stocking

cut two

index